D1435548

Raised by Wolves

Also by Jerome Charyn

Edited by Jerome Charyn

Raised

BY

Wolves

THE TURBULENT ART AND TIMES
OF QUENTIN TARANTINO

JEROME CHARYN

THUNDER'S MOUTH PRESS • NEW YORK

𝕽aised ʙʏ 𝔚olves
The Turbulent Art and Times of Quentin Tarantino

AVALON
publishing group incorporated

Copyright © 2006 by Jerome Charyn

Published by
Thunder's Mouth Press
An Imprint of Avalon Publishing Group
245 West 17th Street, 11th Floor
New York, NY 10011

First printing June 2006

Library of Congress Cataloging-in-Publication Data is available.

ISBN-10: 1-56025-858-6
ISBN-13: 978-1-56025-858-2

9 8 7 6 5 4 3 2 1

Book design by Maria E. Torres
Printed in the United States
Distributed by Publishers Group West

This book is for my three favorite sibyls, Anoosh, Jamie, and Leinana.
And for my research assistant, Mathieu the Magician,
who was able to crawl into every crack and find what I needed to know.

Contents

Introduction

Horses and Rabbit Holes

1.

It was a year ago, perhaps a little more, and I was watching some midnight movie on HBO. Tony Scott's *Crimson Tide* (1995), a doomsday thriller on board a submarine. It's after the breakup of the Soviet Union and Russia is in free fall, caught in the thick of civil war, with an ultranationalist leader threatening to nuke the United States and Japan. Enter the USS *Alabama,* a nuclear sub with enough warheads to destroy a hundred civilizations, old and new. But the real confrontation isn't between ultranationalists and the United States. It's between Gene Hackman and Denzel Washington. Forget the names they're obliged to wear. Hackman is the sub's commander and Washington is his executive officer. Both men have a *weight* on the screen, a density few other actors have. We believe in them no matter what the scenario tells us, no matter how foolish the dialogue or flimsy the tale.

Tony Scott sculpts the submarine in a formidable range of reds and blues, but it's the fury in Hackman's face that holds us. He wants to dismantle the Russians with a nuclear strike, and Denzel Washington won't let him. The chain of command is broken on board the *Alabama,* involved as it is in its own civil war. Denzel Washington seizes the sub. And in the final confrontation between Hackman and him, with officers prepared to blow each other's brains out, Hackman starts talking about Lipizzaner stallions, the prize show horses of Vienna's Spanish Riding School. Hackman says the Lipizzaners are "all white" and come from Portugal. Washington says they aren't from Portugal, but from Spain. "At birth they're not white. They're black." And the duel continues. Horses are only horses, says Hackman. "Stick a cattle prod up its ass, and you can get a horse to deal cards."

Suddenly we've moved from submarines and atomic warfare to a kind of never-never land where anything goes. We're outside the range of Tony Scott's reds and blues. The film has been torpedoed, or rather *tarantinoed.* I could recognize Tarantino's subversive signature even when I was half asleep. His name doesn't appear in the credits, but he had worked on the script. Perhaps the Lipizzaners weren't even his. But that only deepened his influence.

Tarantino has changed cinema, pushed us far from films with a discernible beginning, middle, and end. He's created a chatter, a constant noise that refuses to go away. "You don't really enter a theater" to watch a Tarantino film, "you go down a rabbit hole," according to Janet Maslin. And that rabbit hole consists primarily of talk, as if a hundred Mad Hatters were let loose at a gangsters' convention. Critics keep complaining about the gratuitous violence in Tarantino: violent acts are "just the commas and semicolons of Tarantino's cinematic vocabulary," Daniel Mendelsohn writes in *The New York Review of Books.* And beyond the violence is an emptiness, a passivity, "the sense that you're not in the presence of a creator but of a member of the audience," sitting alone in the dark. It's "as a representative of a generation raised on televised reruns and replays of videotapes that he really scares you to death."

Robin Wood, who's so sensitive to Hitchcock, who can analyze the slightest frisson in *Vertigo,* dismisses Tarantino as a spurious stepchild of the movies, a perpetual adolescent who can only feed back to an audience the image of "its own cleverness, its own emptiness and cynicism." And Roger Shattuck believes that meaningful art "deserves to be protected with all our powers from those [like Tarantino] who would borrow its mantle to protect and ennoble displays of unredeemed depravity and violence."

Yet why do I feel a coherence, a form, a music, where Mendelsohn, Wood, and Shattuck feel none? Why do I sense a deep structure in Tarantino's rabbit hole, where others sense no structure at all? Nothing but the chaotic ramblings of a former video clerk. Tarantino may be the very best *and* worst salesman of himself. The five years he spent behind the counter at Video Archives in the Los Angeles suburb of Manhattan Beach have been mythologized into the most successful crash course in the history of filmmaking. "I'm first and foremost a film geek." That is Tarantino's war cry. "If Quentin didn't make it in the film business, it's very likely he'd have ended up a serial killer," says director Roger Avary, who worked with Tarantino in the same store and would become his writing partner for several years.

"I didn't go to college," says Tarantino. "To me the video store was like my tenure at college . . . when your four years are up, you have to actually start your life, but you end up hanging on to that free zone. Video Archives was my free zone."

This free zone didn't nurture him as much as he thinks. It gave him shelter. He would often sleep in the back of the store. He would find girlfriends on the other side of the counter. He would get into fights. He would even form a kind of guerilla filmmaking unit with fellow clerks. But it didn't challenge him in a fundamental way. That challenge would come from acting school. He'd grown up with the dream of becoming a movie star, and that dream has never left him. "I don't have the fame of a director in America," he said in 1996. "I have the fame of a movie star." But there's a terrible wound behind that bravura: he knows he'll never be a movie star. "A cartoony-looking character with a high forehead and prominent jaw, he [comes] across like Martin Scorsese in the body of Popeye," according to Peter Biskind.

He never even finished the ninth grade. He quit school at sixteen to study acting full time. He chased after roles, but could only land the part of an Elvis Presley impersonator in a single episode of a sitcom. "Well, acting means everything in the world to me. I studied for six years, but I never got any work. I could never get the audition. I tried for years and years to have a career and couldn't get anywhere. Acting taught me everything I know about writing and directing."

He didn't join the Writers Guild or the Directors Guild, even after *Pulp Fiction* made him the most adored screen-writer-director on the planet. But he was a member of the Screen Actors Guild. "You have to join SAG, or you won't be able to work. SAG is the one union I tried for years to join and couldn't get in."

But the old wound wouldn't rub away. "I'm just as serious

about my acting as I am about directing. As I am about writing. I'm as proud of my work acting in *From Dusk Till Dawn* [1996] as I am of my writing and directing in *Pulp Fiction*." Tarantino wrote the screenplay of Robert Rodriguez's film about vampires in a biker bar and plays George Clooney's psychopathic brother with a kind of lunatic lilt.

From Dusk Till Dawn has to be one of the silliest films ever made. But that didn't stop Tarantino. He decided to play the role of another psychopath on Broadway. And actor David Carradine asked him: "Why do you want to parade around on a stage in front of a bunch of blue-haired ladies who arrived on a bus? Because that's what Broadway is."

But his own maniacal belief in himself as an actor is also one of Tarantino's strengths: he directs and writes with an actor's perspective, vulnerability, and point of view. He spent five years studying with Allen Garfield, a character actor from Newark, New Jersey, born in 1939. Garfield, who was trained at the Actors Studio under Lee Strasberg, projects his own brand of comic hostility on screen; one can almost feel him seethe under the skin.

Tarantino was his very first pupil at the Actors' Shelter, which Garfield opened in 1985, with weekend classes at a theater in Beverly Hills. Tarantino was often short of cash and couldn't pay his tuition, but Garfield kept him at the school and would nudge him constantly. "Quentin, you want to be a director? Every time you do a scene in my class, I expect it also to be directed." And Tarantino did as he was told. The Actors' Shelter "was film school as far as I'm concerned." Garfield would become his mentor.

Tarantino wrote "all these rambling, uncharted monologues" for Garfield's class, but that was the beginning of his own craft. The monologue or riff would soon become the basis of his best writing. And monologues from his Actors' Shelter weekends would reappear in *Reservoir Dogs* and *Pulp Fiction,* and in his screenplay for Tony Scott's *True Romance* (1993).

There are riffs about Elvis throughout *True Romance.* Clarence (Christian Slater) is a kind of stand-in for Tarantino himself. He works at his own Video Archives, a comic-book shop called Heroes For Sale. He's an Elvis man. "If I had to fuck a guy, if my life depended on it, I'd fuck Elvis." He falls in love with a call girl, Alabama (Patricia Arquette), who insists: "I'm not Florida white trash." She was paid by Clarence's own boss to give him the ultimate birthday present: a one-night stand. Clarence and 'Bama wake up in the morning and get married. But Clarence cannot bear to learn about her pimp, Drexl, played by Gary Oldman with a menace that's much, much deeper than impersonation: he's a white man with dreadlocks who thinks he's black. Clarence goes to Drexl to demand Alabama's release from her service as a sexual slave. But he wants much more than that. His guardian angel–the ghost of Elvis Presley–tells him that he and 'Bama will never be free until Drexl is dead. Drexl knocks the crap out of Clarence and manages to get himself killed. Clarence escapes with what he thinks is Alabama's clothes, and turns out to be a suitcase full of cocaine.

But the little riffs along the way are nothing compared to the centerpiece of the film, an encounter where Clarence and Alabama are both absent. It's the mother of all riffs, a verbal duel between Christopher Walken and Dennis Hopper, a pair of actors whose own strangeness has defied the cinematic machine; they're monstrosities on the moviehouse wall–character actors posing as stars, each with an anger and an articulation that's unique and always moving. Hopper plays against type in *True Romance*; he isn't the usual *crazy* with a pathological talkiness, a logorrhea that almost breaks our eardrums. He's a quiet man, a security guard who walks around in earlaps, has a big black dog named Rommel. He's Clarence's absent dad, just as Tarantino had an absent dad, a father who got away and didn't even make the tiniest connection to his life.

But Dennis Hopper tries to save his son. Gangsters have come for their suitcase of cocaine. Their chief is Christopher Walken–Don Vincenzo–a mob lawyer who represents Mr. Blue Lou Boyle. As a mouthpiece, he's a man of words. He's eloquent and cruel, and uses language like a rapier. He tells Hopper that he's the Antichrist come to hurt him as he's never been hurt before . . . unless Hopper reveals where Clarence and Alabama are hiding.

"They snatched my narcotics," he says; he's going to have a little Q&A with Hopper and warns him not to lie. "Sicilians are great liars. The best in the world. I'm a Sicilian. And my old man was the world heavyweight champion of Sicilian liars. And from growin' up with him I learned the pantomime. Now there are seventeen different things a guy can do when he lies to give himself away. A guy's got seventeen pantomimes. A woman's got twenty . . . and if ya know them like ya know your face, they beat lie detectors all to hell."

Walken speaks like no other actor in the world, but it's difficult to describe his elocution, his manner of breaking down sentences so that each syllable has its own twisting menace. He does look like the Antichrist in his beautiful scarf and coat. And Hopper seems helpless, all alone, without the same eloquence. But Don Vincenzo falls into the trap of his own song.

"So you're Sicilian, huh?" Hopper says. Don Vincenzo has given him all the opening he needs to spin a tale of his own. "Sicilians were spawned by niggers . . . Hundreds and hundreds of years ago the Moors conquered Sicily. And Moors are niggers. They did so much fuckin' with the Sicilian women, they changed the bloodline forever, from blond hair and blue eyes to black hair and dark skin." Walken laughs, totally bewildered. What else can he do? But Hopper continues his riff. "Sicilians still carry that nigger gene . . . Your ancestors are niggers. You're part eggplant."

His elocution is much stricter, almost mournful: the teller has become one with his tale. Walken kisses Hopper and shoots him in the head. "I haven't killed anybody since nineteen eighty-four."

But Hopper has defeated him; the shooting is a pointless coda, a fake little dazzle of Christopher Walken, the Antichrist. The real violence of the scene is in the recitative of the two men, the collateral damage of their songs.

And we've just witnessed a moment that's so *tarantinesque,* not even Tony Scott's stylistics can ruin it, that incessant play of light and dark, where colors multiply and faces move in and out of shadow. The language fights back against the stylized setting, overpowers it, moves us.

A director himself, Hopper can appreciate the daring of Tarantino's riffs, the uniqueness of having an actor perform recitatives in a film. "A producer looks at a script and says, my god, this is a speech, we can't have this in a movie, cut it down to three lines. But Quentin sets up these incredible imaginary circumstances where it allows you to be able to give speeches."

Hopper sees Tarantino as a visual and verbal magician "putting our culture in a Waring blender and redistributing it as an artistic, entertaining phenomenon," a modern Mark Twain, "dealing with the same things as a couple of guys [Huck Finn and the ex-slave Jim] running away on a riverboat and going down the river on the Mississippi."

And it isn't an idle comparison. The world of Huck and Jim is filled with savage riffs, as they form their own little moral compass on a raft, surrounded by hucksters and violent men.

Huck Finn appears as a grown-up in *Pulp Fiction,* but he's called Captain Koons, an Air Force officer played by Christopher Walken. And this time there's no Dennis Hopper to tame his thunder. He gives one of the funniest uninterrupted riffs the movies have ever seen. It's 1972. Koons has just come back from Nam. He's telling five-year-old Butch about the history of his father's watch. And we don't have Tony Scott's colors to blind us. Tarantino gives us a flattened, washed-out world where everything falls into the background while Koons speaks.

"Hello, little man. Boy, I sure heard a bunch about you. See, I was a good friend of your Daddy's. We were in that Hanoi pit of hell over five years together." The words have a musicality, as if Walken were fingering phrases on a clarinet, stopping and starting at will, sentences breaking down into fragments of their own. The watch appears on screen. It once belonged to Butch's great-granddaddy, who bought it at a general store in Knoxville (where Tarantino himself was born), during World War I. "It was your great-granddaddy's war watch, made by the first company ever to make wrist-watches. Your great-granddaddy wore that watch every day he was in the war." After the war, he put it in an old coffee can . . . until Butch's grandfather, Dane Coolidge, wore it in World War II. He was a Marine who died on Wake Island, but not before he gave that watch to an Air Force gunner, asking him "to deliver to his infant son, who he had never seen in the flesh, his gold watch."

And the watch gathers its own myth from one generation to the next. "This watch. This watch was on your Daddy's wrist when he was shot down over Hanoi . . . The way your Daddy looked at it, that watch was your birthright . . . So he hid it in the one place he knew he could hide somethin'. His ass. Five long years, he wore this watch up his ass." And just before he died of dysentery, he gave the watch to Captain Koons. "I hid this uncomfortable hunk of metal up my ass for two years . . . And now, little man, I give the watch to you."

Koons is a teller of tall tales, but his delivery is so deadpan, so authentic in its odd phrasing, that we believe in the partic-ular odyssey of that war watch, and for a moment *we* become Butch; and Tarantino, with Christopher Walken's help, has performed a singular trick: he has made of language the entire world, and we are all the lost children of Tarantino's tale. By focusing on the watch and Koons, without wavering once, he and his camera take us beyond style and logistics and into artifact. The illusion of the screen is gone; we are right there.

Walken is often disingenuous when he talks about his own career. "I'm a terrible analyzer of what will be good," he admits. "Whenever I think the outcome is going to be good, I'm always wrong." Yet he practiced Captain Koons' monologue for eight weeks, regrouping the words in his own private fashion from his days as a dancer, when he had to count off the cadences. "I'm still counting off dance steps as I cross a room. Two-two four. Three-three four. I'm doing that when I talk." And the same counting "lets you decide what the important word is," outside the "prison" of punctuation. "It might be the noun, it might be the verb. It might be a word you never thought of."

According to Dennis Hopper, Walken "has a pureness to his reading that is almost pre-Stanilavski." But he also has an absolute feel for Tarantino's sense of play, for the illogic of rabbit holes. He couldn't stop laughing as he prepared his monologue about Captain Koons and the peripatetic watch he has to hide in his ass. "I'm a performer who grew up seeing the audience as a character . . . I think people go: 'OK, this is Chris [Christopher Walken]. Chris knows he's in the movie. Chris knows it's not real. Chris is having a good time."

No riff can work without an audience, not even in movieland. And it's this sense of play on both sides of the screen that defines Walken and Tarantino. Walken is a perfect operator in Tarantino's little country of operators, where black horses become white . . . and vice versa.

2.

The most daring thing Tarantino has ever done has little to do with pyrotechnics, such as the twenty-minute swordfight at the House of Blue Leaves in *Kill Bill Vol. 1,* but rather with the contortions Mr. Orange (Tim Roth) has to go through as he prepares his own riff in *Reservoir Dogs.* He's an undercover cop imbedded in a little gang that's about to rob a jewelry store. None of these other "Dogs" really know him, and he has to convince them that he's authentic, that he's the real thing. He has his own personal trainer, someone who teaches him to talk like a hood. Holdaway (Randy Brooks) is a cop who wears a green Chairman Mao cap with a red star. He's Orange's acting coach. Orange's real name is Freddy Newendyke, but the problem is we no longer know what "real" is. All the Dogs have coded names—Mr. Orange, Mr.

Blonde, Mr. White, Mr. Blue . . . But these coded names assume their own personality and power. And Freddy Newendyke becomes the role he has to play: Mr. Orange.

"An undercover cop has got to be Marlon Brando," Holdaway advises him. "To do the job you got to be a great actor. You got to be naturalistic. You got to be naturalistic as hell. If you ain't a great actor you're a bad actor, and bad acting is bullshit on this job." It's much more hazardous than studying with Allen Garfield in Beverly Hills. Lousy acting could also lose him his life.

Holdaway gives Orange his script, an anecdote about a drug deal. Orange immediately balks. "I gotta memorize all this? There's over four fuckin' pages of shit here." He has no concept of how to act, and until he does he will live in a perpetual danger zone. Holdaway tells him he can make up whatever he wants, but he has to remember the details. "It's the details that sell your story." (Just as it's the details that make the camera convincing, that allow us to believe in the narrative that unfolds on the screen.) "Now your story takes place in a men's room. You gotta know if they got paper towels or a blower to dry your hands. You gotta know if the stalls got doors or not. You gotta know if they got liquid soap or that pink granulated powder shit . . . Now what *you* gotta do is take all them details and make 'em your own. The story's gotta be about you, and how you perceived the events that took place. And the way you make it your own is you just gotta keep sayin' it and sayin' it and sayin' it and sayin' it and sayin' it."

And he does. We watch him rehearse. Then he performs his little monologue in front of Holdaway. They're on a rooftop, surrounded by graffiti, and the graffiti almost becomes part of the narrative, as if Orange's words long to dance on a wall.

Then Orange delivers the same monologue to several of the Dogs. He could be at an audition, one of Tarantino's own auditions. But Orange can't afford to fail. He talks about lugging around a load of marijuana. He's about to make a sale. But he has to take a leak and he goes into the "little boys room." Suddenly the tale takes on its own logic. And we *see* him in the men's room at a train station, as if the lie he tells has its particular truth: the story is stronger than the undercover cop who tells it. Four Los Angeles County sheriffs and their German shepherd are in the men's room, caught up in their own narrative. They stop talking, look at Orange. The dog barks. "He's barkin' at me. I mean it's obvious he's barkin' at me."

Orange savors the "romance" of his terror. "Every nerve ending, all my senses, the blood in my veins, everything I had was screaming, 'Take off, man, just take off, get the fuck outa there.' Panic hit me like a bucket of water. . . .

And all those sheriffs are lookin' at me and they know. They can smell it. As sure as the fuckin' dog can, they can smell it on me."

The frame freezes, with Orange and his shoulder bag of marijuana in front of the four sheriffs and the dog; it's as if the camera were waiting for the tale to continue, as if the absence of words could stop time and all movement; and then the frame "jerks to life." We hear the dog bark. One of the sheriffs continues his own spiel about a man who nearly got his head blown off. Orange pretends to pee. He walks past the sheriffs to wash his hands in the sink. He turns on the drying machine. The noise of the machine overpowers the frame, becomes a kind of sound track: the world moves into slow motion, caught in the sound of the machine. The dog barks at Orange, but we cannot hear him. The "detail" of the drying machine dominates the story.

The machine turns off, and we move back into "real" time. Orange walks out of the men's room. His riff has ended, and the teller is removed from his own tale. The audition is over. The Dogs congratulate him. He's become one of them. "That's how you do it, kid," says Joe Cabot, leader of the gang. "You knew how to handle that situation. You shit your pants, and then you just dive in and swim."

Orange has taken them in, fooled them all, but at a price. He's no longer Freddy Newendyke; he's the Dogs' own

Marlon Brando. And in the process, Tarantino has revealed the most revolutionary aspect of his art. Words take on a totemic power, almost defy the images on the screen . . . or rule them. In Tarantino's rabbit hole, sight and sound are reversed: we have to "see" with our ears and "hear" with our eyes. Or, as film critic Gavin Smith says: ". . . spectacle and action paradoxically take the form of dialogue and monologue. The verbal setpiece takes precedence over the action setpiece."

And the action itself, whatever we think is "real" on screen, grows out of "verbal constructs." Characters become "what they say—and they never stop talking."

As Tim Roth himself says about Mr. Orange: "I like the idea of being a fiction within a fiction. I'm a liar. I'm creating my own fiction within a fiction, a lie within a lie."

Roth also realized he was entering the rabbit hole. "[Tarantino's script] reminded me of playing, just like being a little kid. It's like, if I'm gonna be in this film, it'd be like all the things I imagined I was gonna do as a kid with a gun in the backyard."

Those critics who accuse Tarantino of being a vampire without emotions, a geek who steals from other films, a rip-off artist who builds his vocabulary on the backs of other filmmakers, ought to look again. Tarantino has taken us on a voyage where *only* an actor could be at the helm, a failed actor who's rendering the metaphysics of monologues he himself had prepared—all the heartbreak of rehearsal. And this provides the pathos for Orange's monologue, where acting is all, a necessary survival kit, as it must have seemed to the gawky boy who quit high school to become an actor. We may be ambivalent about the Dogs and the violence that surrounds them, but we are just as ambivalent about a betrayer in their midst. Yet we're still absorbed in Mr. Orange's quest, in his need for narrative. And *his* rehearsal is about the rehearsal of film itself, the tentativeness of story, any story, as words become pictures on a wall. Had Tarantino not gone to acting school, Orange's tale might have become simple bravura and bluff. But his own transformation into an actor moves us and stuns us, because he's reliving the cinematic machine, the camera's ability to film "a lie within a lie," and Tarantino's ability to layer these lies with his own "left turns," unexpected areas where few filmmakers would dare to go. "Storytelling is cinematic," he says. "Storytelling is seductive, sexy, you know." That's because Tarantino isn't frightened of the void. *Reservoir Dogs* is a heist film without a heist. He leaves great big empty spaces and holes and covers them over with talk as we move from Mad Hatter to Mad Hatter, delighting us as they deliver one madcap monologue after another.

Tarantino wanted *True Romance* to be his first film, but he couldn't finance it, couldn't get it made. His own script was much less linear—a tale within a tale, with multiple time frames—than the script that was finally shot. And we can only wonder about the film Tarantino might have made. "I see my films as canvasses where I fill in the various colors, emotional and visual," says Tony Scott, but Tarantino's canvasses are coloring books filled with words.

Scott admits that Tarantino would have made "a very different *True Romance*—tougher, edgy, less dreamlike, less self-conscious." Scott sees himself as "a hired gun" who has moved from genre to genre, project to project, studio to studio, bringing along his own sense of "style" to whatever film he's working on. But Tarantino has never been "a hired gun," even if his own success has made him into a kind of movie mogul.

Tarantino admires *True Romance*. "I love the way he [Tony Scott] shoots; it's just not my way. He uses a lot of smoke and I don't want any smoke in my movies. I have a lot of long takes, whereas for Tony a long take is twenty seconds." Scott's films often drown in "atmosphere," but he has no real aesthetic. We have no sense of obsession as he moves from film to film, no interior life or "esoteric structure," as film theorist Peter Wollen reminds us. "[Jean] Renoir once remarked that a director spends his whole life making one film." This film "consists not only of the typical features of its variants . . . but of the principle of variation which governs it, that is it's esoteric structure, which can only . . . 'seep to the surface,' in [Claude] Lévi-Strauss's phrase," through a process of repetition.

And whatever we think of Tarantino himself, *Reservoir Dogs* is a film with a controlling vision. It doesn't unfold or "develop" like most studio films. It's like a bit of miraculous light coming out of a black hole. "To spend time with Tarantino," writes film critic J. Hoberman, "is to observe the violence of his own imagination," an imagination that seems to occupy corners rather than some safe middle ground, that bites at us, teases us, frightens and amuses us at the same time, as we jump from riff to riff and watch black horses turn to white.

3.

Harvey Keitel, without whom *Reservoir Dogs* could never have been made, compares Tarantino to Martin Scorsese. "To me there is a common denominator between Quentin and Marty . . . there's a certain intensity these [two] people have, a certain vulnerability, a certain insight." He's Scorsese's monstrous twin. Both of them are wired up, motormouths who talk a mile a minute, like lost boys in a fun house of film. Tarantino considers *Taxi Driver* (1976) to be one of the films that helped form him, but *Taxi Driver* is about silence, crippling isolation, and *Reservoir Dogs* is about song, about language that provides a constant community to a band of lowlifes. Scorsese was a shy, asthmatic child who thought of becoming a priest, but went to film school instead. He is a "classicist" compared to Tarantino, who never even learned to tell time . . .

Tarantino was raised by his mother, who protected his willfulness. "He's a genius, who gives a shit if he can tell time or not?" He would find his own spiritual father in Howard Hawks, whose films taught him a sense of right and wrong and took him into the wonder of storytelling. Hawks possessed him to such a degree, Tarantino dreamt about being invited to his house. "Robert Mitchum was on a balcony and said, 'You're here to see the old man.' Hawks was on a patio with John Wayne. He said, 'Hey, Quentin, come down, kid.' I woke up. I was sad, it was so real."

Tarantino also admires Brian De Palma, John Woo, Sergio Leone, and Jean-Luc Godard, but he doesn't really resemble them or Howard Hawks, who died in 1977 when Tarantino was thirteen. He likes to see himself as a subterranean novelist. "I'm not ragging on screenwriters, but if I was a full-on writer, I'd write novels." And as he admits, the structure of *Reservoir Dogs* and *Pulp Fiction* depends more on the novel than on the mechanics of film. He may hurl his characters across time and space, but there are "no flashbacks, just chapters. . . . The way it is in a novel."

The first novelist he ever read was Elmore Leonard. In fact, he almost went to jail over Leonard when he was fifteen. He was caught swiping Leonard's novel, *The Switch,* at Kmart. The novel is about two ne'er-do-well crooks, Ordell Robbie and Louis Gara, who can't even collect on a kidnapping scheme. Ordell and Louis appear again in *Rum Punch* (1992), the novel that Tarantino would adapt and turn into *Jackie Brown* (1997). But Ordell and Louis don't delight us half as much as Mr. Orange or Captain Koons; they may have their own jargon, but never their own riffs. Tarantino claims that he was influenced by Leonard when he wrote *True Romance*– the screenplay begins in Detroit, where Leonard has lived since he was nine, and ends in LA, Tarantino's own turf–but there's nothing in *The Switch* or *Rum Punch* that equals the "duel" between Christopher Walken and Dennis Hopper, and Hopper's rendering of the Moors in Sicily. What troubles me most about *Jackie Brown* is the utter absence of monologue. The characters move in a slow-motion world without riffs. The inventive play is gone. The pair of dumb cops who try to nail Jackie remain dull, because they have no language that really interests us. They are never defined by talk, but by their snickers and snorts, and they aren't funny enough to be part of Tarantino's own little menagerie. Leonard's characters inhabit a much more "naturalistic" landscape. And Tarantino might never admit it, but he'd outgrown Leonard by the time he wrote *Jackie Brown. His* talk wears a subtle flesh. *His* stories take on "a lot more resonance being told in this kind of like wild way," as he said to Charlie Rose. And Tarantino's way is wilder than Elmore Leonard's.

The creator he most resembles is novelist James Ellroy. Both of them are Los Angeles brats, and both use that city as a mythological backdrop in their very best work. Los Angeles is a kind of anti–New York, a city that has no real center and is a series of neighborhoods on route to some highway by the sea. It's anonymous, amorphous, full of camouflage, so that we can hide in plain sight and become our very own chameleon. If New York is defined by the number and variety of its "Ramblas," avenues where we can meet all manner of civilizations face-to-face, Los Angeles has its freeways, which carry us from neighborhood to neighborhood, from bohemian enclaves to rich and poor ghettos. People without wheels are considered Martians or worse.

Los Angeles and its suburbs by the sea, like Manhattan Beach and Torrance, where Tarantino grew up, are emblematic of modern life, where places become "no place," and where the psyche has to define itself against a void, an invisible culture in which faces disappear and then reappear in

some different landscape, like the panels of George Her-
riman's comic strip, *Krazy Kat,* where Krazy will move from
the desert to the ocean or a brick wall while continuing the
same conversation.

And this sense of *displacement* is like a wound in Tarantino
and Ellroy, where Los Angeles masquerades as a home that
can never be home. Tarantino and Ellroy are vagabonds,
wanderers in LA. Ellroy's wound is more obvious and much
worse. His mom, Geneva Odelia Hilliker Ellroy, or Jean, a
redhead with hazel eyes, was murdered, strangled to death,
when he was a boy of ten, a fifth-grader, "a frightened and
rather volatile child. " At first he was *almost* glad. His mom,
who was divorced from his dad, Armand Ellroy, an
accountant who was "drop-dead handsome," had brought
him from Santa Monica to El Monte, a "shitkicker town" in
the San Gabriel Valley, "White Trash Heaven." He raged
against the loss of his mother. "I hated her. I hated El Monte.
Some unknown killer just bought me a brand-new beautiful
life." He moved in with Armand. He became a reader the
summer Jean died, shoplifting books to augment his little
library of adolescent detective tales. "Every book I read was
a twisted homage to her. Every mystery solved was my love
for her in ellipses."

He idolized his dad who had once been Rita Hayworth's
personal manager. But Armand could barely take care of

himself. He was about fifty years older than the boy, looked like his granddad. Ellroy had to steal food or he and his dad would have starved. "We were poor . . . We wore ratty clothes." Like Tarantino, he had "poor hygiene" and would become "a teenage leper." He enlisted in the army at seventeen, and realized that soldiering wasn't for him. He started to stutter. "I was a Method actor tapping into real-life resources . . . My long twitchy body was a great actor's tool."

The army let him go. He became a burglar and a common thief. He would steal into the homes of women he knew, pocketing their panties and bras. "Burglary was voyeurism multiplied a thousand times." He lived out on the street like a half-tamed wolf and spent his days reading in public libraries. He was in and out of jail, became an alcoholic, like his mom and dad. "Jail was my health retreat," jail cleaned him up. He began to hallucinate. He smoked pot. "It was like trying to reach the moon in a Volkswagen."

Hospitalized, broken, with an abscess on his left lung the size of a fist, he still had a crazy optimism. "I possessed a self-preserving streak at the height of my self-destruction. My mother gave me the gift and the curse of obsession." And this obsession would carry him into writing books, books that were disguised portraits of his mother, remembrances and dreams. "I didn't know that storytelling was my only true voice. . . . Narrative was my moral language." And he had his own theme, one enormous vision, to reconstruct LA around his mother's death. "I wanted to canonize the secret LA I first glimpsed the day the redhead died."

Ellroy became the poet of a "White Bread Heaven" that had engulfed Jean, devoured her. He would render his own version of "white jazz." And this is the *music* we hear again and again in *Reservoir Dogs* and *True Romance,* the songs of assorted lowlifes. Ellroy's novels often read like long extended riffs. And as Tarantino grew famous, he began to mythologize himself, reconstruct his past, pretend he'd come from Ellroy's "hillbilly heaven," a product of "trailer trash," but he wasn't. His upbringing was decidedly middle class. His mother provided him with whatever he wished, from GI Joe dolls to board games and books. Yet Tarantino was drawn to the "white trash" and black, Latino, and Samoan culture of Carson City, where his favorite moviehouse was located, the Carson Twin Cinema. "I was hassled by the cops," he says. "I looked like white trash. I never went anywhere. I never left Los Angeles County."

Like Ellroy, he was tall for his age—both of them were well over six feet by the time they were fifteen, both of them had a crazy streak, a bit of menace in their blood. Tarantino's manager, Cathryn Jaymes, saw in him "a combination of Elvis and Charles Manson." And Tarantino liked to boast of the alternative career he might have had. "If I hadn't wanted to make movies, I would have ended up as Ordell [Ordell Robbie in *Jackie Brown*]. I wouldn't have been a postman or worked in the phone company or been a salesman or a guy selling gold by the inch. I would have been involved with one scam after another. I would have gone to jail." Tarantino did do time in LA County Jail, but only for traffic ticket violations. He wasn't a burglar, like Ellroy, though he would have an abiding sympathy for thieves and the world of thieves, and it's this sympathy that empowers *Reservoir Dogs,* rather than an impersonal gift for being able to mimic a Mr. White or Mr. Blonde. He also has Ellroy's stubbornness, that need to narrate. He approaches acting, writing, and directing with the tenacity of a safecracker. "I never set up a fall-back situation because I didn't want to fall back . . . I wanted to keep eating at it," he told Charlie Rose. And he did.

Ellroy lost his mother in a traumatic, shocking way, and he had to become a father to his own father, steal food in order to keep them alive. Tarantino seems to have had no father. "I—I only have a mom," he told one film critic. "I never met my real father," he told another. His mother, Connie, left his father, Tony Tarantino, a law student and a struggling actor, well before Quentin was born. Connie had zeroed Tony Tarantino out of her life, hurled him into the shadows. "[Quentin's] like *me.* He looks like *me.*" She would take Quentin to the movies, not to watch kiddie films or some cartoon festival. He saw *Carnal Knowledge* by the time he was six . . .

If Jean Ellroy's absence and ghostly presence defines the art of her son, if his novels are love-and-hate songs to her, Connie's *material* presence (and the invisibility of his father) would play an enormous part in Tarantino's films. The all-male ensemble of petty gangsters in *Reservoir Dogs* provides Tarantino with a multitude of dads. And Jackie Brown is as much a veiled portrait of his own mom—a strong and sexy mama who can get out of *any* predicament—as it is an homage to the foxiness of Pam Grier. The Bride (Uma Thurman) in *Kill Bill* is a resourceful killing machine who has inherited much of Connie's own stamina and flair. (She's also inherited the black and red pens that Tarantino uses to write all his scripts; The Bride keeps a strict accounting of the "vipers" she has killed with Tarantino's pens).

Ellroy and Tarantino are autodidacts who seized upon their own education; language itself became a kind of quest. They are both lovers of "pulp fiction," of popular forms that resist inter-pretation, that mock mainstream culture, that have the rawness and energy of *everyday* madness. They are crime writers who see an essential poetry in the language of lowlifes. They're lone wolves who arrived without antecedents, who shaped them-selves out of uncertainty, yet seemed certain of their craft.

"Quentin came out of the box already on fire," says Bruce

Willis. And his handicap of being unable to spell hasn't harmed him. "Quentin's strength comes from his ability to write although he really has no ability to *physically* write," says Roger Avary. "Quentin writes phonetically . . . It's a bit of a mess." But it's this *phonetic* writing that has helped capture voices and sounds that seem to rise up from the interior landscape of his characters, that's close to dream language, a dream language that actors such as Tim Roth and Christopher Walken can articulate with their own strange diction.

And we mustn't forget Tarantino's notebooks and his black and red pens. "I don't know how to type properly. When I know I'm going to do a script, I'll go to a stationery store and buy a notebook . . . and I'll say, 'OK, this is the notebook I'm going to write *Pulp Fiction* or whatever in. I also buy three red felt pens and three black felt pens. I make this big ritual out of it . . . I can take this notebook places. I can write in restaurants, I can write in friends' houses, I can write standing up, I can write lying down in my bed—I can write everywhere. It never looks like a script; it always looks like . . . the diary of a madman."

It may be "all chicken scratch," as director Alexandre Rockwell says about Tarantino's scripts, but his chicken scratch—his diary of a madman—has taken us into a rabbit hole where in all the odd distortions we can often find a reflection of our own faces.

CHAPTER ONE

Raised by Wolves

1.

In *Li'l Abner,* created by Al Capp, there's a comic strip within the comic strip about Fearless Fosdick, a feckless cop who is always being attacked and shot at, the bullets whizzing through his body, leaving round holes that can't hurt him and are like a trademark. In the middle of some misadventure, Li'l Abner can be found under a tree, perusing his favorite "comical book," in which Fearless' misadventures become his own. Li'l Abner is a loveable lout, a giant with the eagerness and mental capacities of a ten-year-old. He lives in a hillbillyland called Dogpatch. If Li'l Abner can enter whatever "comical book" he's reading, one can also imagine Fearless inhabiting a world outside comic books. He could almost fit into Tarantino's landscapes, a hillbilly cop chasing other hillbillies . . .

One might also imagine Tarantino as Li'l Abner, an infectious giant who hasn't lost any of a child's enthusiasm. Even at forty, he watches films like a little boy. Being president of the jury didn't stop him from throwing himself into every film he watched at the 2004 Cannes Film Festival. "We're supposed to be subtle, stone-faced," says director Jerry Schatzberg, who was on the same jury. But Tarantino wasn't subtle at all. "When the fight scenes are going on [in a film], he's fighting, he's doing it. He starts applauding. He's laughing, fighting: he becomes part of the film. He's living it. . . . A lot of the time he can't control his emotions."

Schatzberg first met him at another festival in 1994, and he doesn't see much of a difference in Tarantino. "He has the same enthusiasm, maybe more."

It's as if he's kept Li'l Abner's innocence and charm in spite of the fact that he can maneuver so well among moguls. "There is still something gawky and virginal about Tarantino," writes Larissa MacFarquhar in a *New Yorker* profile about him. And Dogpatch has become part of his own personal myth, particularly his childhood, which has so many variants and versions that he seems to have hidden among the "trailer trash" of Knoxville, Tennessee, and the suburban beach towns near Los Angeles International Airport.

But there were no Pappy or Mammy Yocums in his childhood, even if several critics have talked about moonshining grandparents and an unconventional mom, a teenage bride who carried him across the country in a papoose and wore out six pairs of moccasins, considering that she's part Cherokee.

"I *am* half Cherokee," says Connie, "but you wouldn't know it, that's just sensationalism—I did not walk across the United States in moccasins. The only reason I was in Tennesse when Quentin was born was because I was in college then."

There couldn't have been a grandpa who sold moonshine, since Connie's own dad died when she was an infant. "Quentin will have you believe he was raised by wolves." But perhaps he was, at least by the wolves of his own imagination.

"[Quentin's] always driving forward with a very positive kind of outlook," says Alexandre Rockwell. "The articles that have been written about him say he had some Li'l Abner upbringing or something, but his mother isn't like that and Quentin isn't like that. Of course, there's probably some darkness in there, because he drives toward being positive to the point where you feel there's something chasing him. I mean, you feel that there's *something* that frightens him."

But whatever is chasing him is hard to catch. He's modulated his own terrors, used them in his work to such a degree that John Travolta has said: "I can't find his fear." And Jerry Schatzberg, Uma Thurman, and others have described him as "fearless."

Perhaps we ought to consider Tarantino as a weaver of fairy tales, with a child's weaknesses and many, many strengths, with its belief in danger lurking everywhere, as giants *and* wolves want to swallow it alive, and violence is a daily occurrence, one more thing in the atmosphere. Tarantino himself has talked about the danger his *Reservoir Dogs* were in: "Violence was like another character in the room. It hung over the proceedings." Scatology is also omnipresent in his films; he's like a child testing barriers and breaking taboos. And we ought to listen to Tarantino when he says that *Abbott and Costello Meet Frankenstein* (1948) is his favorite film *after* Howard Hawks's *Rio Bravo* (1959). His devotion to Hawks's comical bunch of cowboys is clear enough. Hawks destroys the myth of the Western as a child might do. Yet, for Tarantino, *Abbott and Costello Meet Frankenstein* shatters certain shibboleths—it insists that comedy and terror are often inseparable, part of the very same structure in a child's nervous system, where you move from one to the other without a blink. First "you're at the funny part, then you're at the scary part, then you're at the funny part again." Or, as Tarantino would say about *Reservoir Dogs:* "I like the idea that the audience is laughing and that, BOOM, the next moment there is blood on the walls. Then there are more laughs."

Every single film he saw excited him at an early age. And

he's held on to the magic and wonderment that these films delivered, reluctant to give them up. His inability to write—his chicken scratch—or tell time is part of the same insistence to retain a child's mysteries and magic rites. There must have been something so *problematic* about his childhood, with or without the Li'l Abner stories, that film became his safety net. And this is what separates him from most other filmmakers— the very act of watching a film, with his hyena laugh and his absolute involvement in the action, was a matter of life and death.

2.

Tarantino's mom, Connie McHugh, was born in Tennessee on September 3, 1946. She had a peripatetic childhood, wandering everywhere. ". . . my mother was always running off doing different things and I preferred my grandmother and my aunt." By age six she was living in Cleveland with another set of parents, Betty and Ellen Schaffer. But her wanderlust didn't end there. She moved to Southern California after finishing junior high, lived with an aunt, and graduated from high school at fifteen. She was resourceful, intelligent, and high-strung. "Everyone else was going away to college," and Connie was like a brainy Cinderella who had to be home by ten. But she was still too young to live on her own. While riding at a local stable, she met Tony Tarantino, a twenty-year-old law student and would-be actor, and married him. She had an "accidental" pregnancy. "I was so angry over being pregnant because he had told me he couldn't have children." Connie returned to Tennessee without Tony and started college. She was sixteen and studying microbiology and nursing in Knoxville when Quentin was born on March 27, 1963.

The myth of Quentin Jerome Tarantino began even before his birth. His very naming is problematic. "Quentin" or "Quint" comes from two sources: William Faulkner and TV. Connie was fond of Quint Asper, a halfbreed Indian black-smith played by Burt Reynolds on *Gunsmoke*, the most pop-ular TV serial of the fifties and sixties. She was also a fan of *The Sound and the Fury*, and was moved by Quentin Compson and his niece, who was named after him, and who was as high-strung as Connie herself. "I decided when I was preg-nant that whether he was a boy or a girl his name was going to be Quentin." *The Sound and the Fury*, with its shattered time frames, would serve Tarantino's own sense of fragmentation in *Reservoir Dogs* and *Pulp Fiction*, with their "chapters" that shove all over the place.

Little Quentin went to live with his grandmother while Connie finished college. She moved back to Southern Cali-fornia and sent for Quentin after six months. He'd been a kind of superbaby, with Connie's own willfulness, and now he was two and a half. She married a local musician, Curtis Zastoupil, who adopted the little boy. Connie's brother and Curt's brother also lived with them for a while; and Quentin Tarantino, now Quentin Zastoupil, was surrounded by uncles and a stepfather who rarely worked, while Connie was building her career as an executive at an HMO. But she also spent a lot of time with "Q," as she called him, taking him to the movies. Connie felt that she was as much a child as Quentin when they watched *Carnal Knowledge* or *Bambi*. Both of them were terrorized by the death of Bambi's mother. There was an odd relationship between mother and son, almost as if she were an older sister who'd had such an aborted childhood (a bride and a mother at sixteen), and was reliving her childhood with him, even though she had to support Quentin *and* Curt.

Curt himself was more like an older brother than a stepfather, and would be out of Quentin's life soon enough (Connie divorced him when "Q" was nine or ten). Yet Tarantino would mythologize Curt in his own curious way. Curt's relatives, Aunt Ginny and Uncle Conrad, also belong to Jimmie of Toluca Lake, the character Tarantino plays in *Pulp Fiction:* he didn't give up his relatives lightly. But the most important "relative," his own father, Tony Tarantino, had become a no-no and was never discussed, until "Q" would say that he *only* had a mom. Yet his invisible dad must have marked him. The most tender and touching portrait in all his work is that of Clifford Worley (Dennis Hopper), Clarence's dad in *True Romance*. Cliff, who lives in a trailer park, is a "lost" father in his own little lost world. And the dialogue between father and son seems to come from a different part of the psyche than the usual biting reports of Tarantino's other characters; a nerve is touched, and for a moment we're outside comedy and menace.

Cliff seems to be talking about Tarantino himself when he says to Clarence: "You're your fucking mother through and through. I haven't heard from you in three years. Then you show up all of a sudden at eight o'clock in the morning. You walk in like a goddamn bulldozer . . . don't get me wrong, I'm happy to see you . . . just slow it down."

And the motormouth tells him about the trouble he's in— the corpse he's left behind (Drexl), and the cocaine he happened to grab from Blue Lou Boyle. An ex-cop, Cliff gets whatever information he can. And when Dennis Hopper says, "I love you, son," lines he's rarely delivered on screen, we can feel the underpull of emotion. Clarence and Alabama go off to California on their honeymoon (with the cocaine). Enter Don Vincenzo (Christopher Walken). And to prevent himself from being tortured into betraying his son, Cliff performs his monologue about Sicilians and their "nigger gene," knowing that Don Vincenzo will kill him right away . . .

Whatever Tarantino has borrowed, stolen, or cannibalized from novelists and other filmmakers, this moment is entirely his own. It's the remembrance of a child, coded somewhere, about a father he wasn't allowed to have but could store in the inventory of his imagination. And the meeting between father and son has an alchemy we seldom find in any film.

Part of the problem that Tarantino had as a little boy was this profusion of males (without a real father) and a mom who overwhelmed him. "He loved kindergarten," Connie said. "Then it was all downhill." But kindergarten is about play rather than learning by rote. He began to falter in first and second grade. "Something misfired there." He was stuck, couldn't really progress, as if time had frozen around him, and he would remain a little boy—dysfunctional, his teachers called him, hyperactive. But it's actor Steve Buscemi rather than some child psychologist who best captures Tarantino's dilemma. "When I saw *Pulp Fiction,* the little boy [young Butch] watching the big TV, being alone in the room, the TV being his friend—to me that's Quentin."

This is the same scene where Captain Koons (Christopher Walken) tells the boy about his dead father's gold watch. At the beginning of the scene the boy is watching *Clutch Cargo,* one of the strangest and most haunting cartoons ever to appear on television; it featured "limited animation," in which only a character's lips moved; otherwise it was one still image after another. In a process called "Syncro-Vox," human lips were superimposed over the mouths of zombie-like characters. Clutch Cargo was a hopscotching pilot who had a little freckle-faced ward, Skinner, with a dog named Paddlefoot.

We never meet Clutch, only his adopted son, who looks like a ventriloquist's dummy with freckles, a wooden boy with phantom lips. Skinner has a spooky resemblance to Tarantino when he would play with GI Joe and Spiderman dolls and have the dolls speak, using the curse words he must have picked up from his uncles and stepfather. And he would apologize to Connie. "It wasn't me, Mommy. It was GI Joe and Spiderman talking to Batman."

He'd become both the ventriloquist and the dummy; and at some point, with a bit of creative schizophrenia, he couldn't tell the difference. This acting out would serve him well when he began writing screenplays and could assume so many voices, whether Batman or Mr. Blonde. But the screenplays were done in that same childish script, as if he refused to learn *or* recognize any signs other than his own. He's been collecting dolls—often huge—all his life. He also collects board games and comic books. The apartments he's had were cluttered with them, and with a six-month supply of Yoo-hoo, a devilishly sweet chocolate drink favored by children and childlike adults.

Tarantino's first biographer, Jami Bernard, talks about his devotion to "the detritus of childhood." For a while he wouldn't travel anywhere without his dolls. He once stayed in the apartment of Alexandre Rockwell and his wife, actress Jennifer Beals. "You didn't want to go into the room he was staying in, 'cause it was like a pop media bomb went off, with half-drunk Dr Peppers, board games, full-sized John Travolta dolls," Rockwell remembers.

But it's this very clutter–the dream and debris of childhood–that has been the touchstone of Tarantino's art. His own childlike qualities have kept him innocent *and* brutal, like a fairy-tale king in command of characters who talk with the urgency of children. They bark out whatever madness is inside their heads and inhabit some primordial cave like Jack Rabbit Slim's, the retro diner in *Pulp Fiction* that resembles a movie palace raised to monstrous proportions, where artifacts take over and imprison the humans who wander into it, turn them into dolls . . .

3.

Tarantino's situation at school would get worse and worse. He had to repeat the ninth grade, and finally at fifteen or sixteen he quit school. He wanted to *animate* the voices inside his dolls, become an actor, but Connie insisted that he also find a job. He became an usher at the Pussycat, a porn theater in Torrance. He was six foot two and could handle himself, but he was perhaps the only one inside the theater who didn't like porn. The films were sleazy to him, without that dreamlike play of characters involved in their own whirlwind. And most of all, they weren't funny.

Once he was away from school, Connie couldn't really control him. "It was at the point where the horse was out the barn door." He was also in the midst of some metamorphosis, toying with new names for himself, like "Quint Jerome." He certainly couldn't act under his legal name, Quentin Zastoupil. The kids at school had called him "Disaster-Pill." He got rid of "Disaster-Pill" and took back "Tarantino." He enrolled at the James Best Theater Company in Toluca Lake.

It was 1981, and he was Li'l Abner with a lantern jaw. "Jimmie" Best had worked with director Sam Fuller, "one of the greatest wild men of cinema." Fuller's rough-and-tumble style would help shape Tarantino as a filmmaker. Best had appeared in *Verboten!* (1959) and *Shock Corridor* (1963), two films that reject the Hollywood notion of "seamless" storytelling and take us to the edge of chaos. But Fuller never had a wide appeal, and it was television that brought Jimmie Best a bit of fame. He played a bumbling sheriff, Rosco P.

Coltrane, in *The Dukes of Hazzard* (1979–1985). Hazzard County, Georgia, is the closest thing to Dogpatch, a hillbilly-land where a family of former moonshiners, the Dukes, fight against a corrupt commissioner and his imbecilic sidekicks. *The Dukes of Hazzard* was also one of the board games that Tarantino would collect. And he would bring Jimmie Best into his menagerie by calling a character in *Pulp Fiction* "Jimmie of Toluca Lake"–a character played by Tarantino himself.

He had his own problems at the James Best Theater Company: ". . . little by little I realized that I didn't fit in with the rest of the actors in the school. I was too movie-mad, and my idols weren't other actors. My idols were directors like Brian De Palma. I decided I didn't want to be in movies, I wanted to make movies."

Tarantino switched schools, studied with Allen Garfield, who encouraged him to direct. "It was so cool because I could direct scenes in his class." And it was Garfield who first saw Tarantino's "triple threat"–as an actor, writer, and director, but one who wouldn't "flounder" like Orson Welles, with a brilliance that "just surfaced every once in a while after his first hurrah."

After he left the Pussycat and endured "this little stupid job here and that little stupid job there," he stumbled upon his own little Xanadu–Video Archives, "a magnet for every movie geek in the South Bay," according to Peter Biskind. Lance Lawson, owner of the store, recalls the first time Tarantino appeared at Video Archives. It was 1983, and Tarantino was twenty. "He came by as a film buff one day, and we started talking about movies and got into a discussion about Brian De Palma. Four hours later we were still talking."

Soon Lawson hired him at four dollars an hour, and Lawson's entire stock was now a moveable feast, since Tarantino could take home as many videos as he liked. The store itself would become his home. "I basically lived there for years. We'd get off work, close up the store, then sit around and watch movies all night."

He would form his own "Reservoir Dogs" with the other video clerks, who had a lot of Tarantino's ambition. Critics such as Peter Biskind have romanticized his relation to the store, believing that Tarantino emerged "like an exotic butterfly, out of the Archives cocoon." But Tarantino was an exotic butterfly long before Video Archives. He was writing stories by the time he was ten, even if he was the only person on the planet who could understand his "chicken scratch." He was *always* writing, his mother remembers. "Every year I'd get a Mother's Day story. But he would always kill me off in the story."

Video Archives extended his habitat, gave him his own little company of geeks. Fellow clerks such as Roger Avary,

Stephen Polyi, and Gerald Martinez were like rival siblings, siblings he'd never had, in another fatherless universe, since Lance Lawson was absent much of the time. Tarantino was helpless . . . and tyrannical. The "Archives Dogs" had to watch over him. "He had no concept of numbers or mathematics or even east or west—you can't give him directions, you have to take him by the hand and show him," said Stephen Polyi. And the "Dogs" had to get him out of jail when the cops caught up with him and his supposedly seven thousand dollars worth of traffic tickets. But Tarantino wasn't the typical fanboy. When a customer wanted to know about a film, he would act out entire scenes; he knew the décor and the dialogue by heart. "This is one of the few places where Quentin could come as a regular guy and get a job, and still be a star," said Martinez. "Because he was like, 'the star of the store.' "

He considered himself the Pauline Kael of Video Archives. The boy who was raised by wolves, read like a wolf, with a wolf's endless appetite. Even during his days as a video clerk, he would unplug his phone and go "underground," with his nose inside a book. "I like to read. It's almost like sex in a relationship—you have to keep on it, or you won't do it."

He started reading Pauline Kael at sixteen. "I've read everything she's ever written for *The New Yorker* and got all her books, and I've learned as much from her as I have from filmmakers. She taught me a sense of how to be dramatically engaging, how to make a connection with the audience. She was my professor."

Such has been the success surrounding Tarantino after *Pulp Fiction*—the first independent film ever to make over a hundred million dollars—that critics have come to see him as the guru of a new video-store culture, where a whole band of ex-clerks, including Roger Avary and Kevin Smith, have become filmmakers. Smith's *Clerks* (1994) features a video clerk who opens and closes whenever he's in the mood. The film is funny, sad, and foulmouthed, and offers us a glimpse of a New Jersey wasteland, in black and white (actually Smith himself had clerked at a convenience store, which is the main locale of the film). But suddenly there was a "rush" about filmmakers who hadn't gone to NYU, UCLA, or USC, as Oliver Stone, Steven Spielberg, Martin Scorsese, Francis Ford Coppola, and George Lucas had done.

The band of ex-clerks had a spokesman in Roger Avary, who articulated its needs and desires. Two years younger than Tarantino, Avary was born in Canada. He studied film at the Art Center College of Design in Pasadena, but dropped out. Video Archives gave him all the film culture he required. "Why go to film school to listen to somebody lecture about film in the old style when you can sit around for eight or ten hours a day and discuss movies with your friends. That was the greatest film school any of us could ever know."

When video came along with its own avatar, the video store, "a culture of scarcity was transformed, almost overnight, into a culture of plenty," thus "stripping film of its hieratic halo, the mystique of the image" that had once been like an act of faith to French and American auteurs and critics, from François Truffaut to Martin Scorsese and Arthur Penn. Video brought a "Reformation," making film schools and all the teacher-priests attached to the "religion of cinema" obsolete, writes Peter Biskind.

"There's a fresh generation of filmmakers, and they're coming out of the video stores," says Roger Avary, with thousands of movies that one can conjure right off the shelves. And then came the new mystique—that video, television, comic books, and board games offered a more profound sweep of the culture and a livelier language than any strict interpretation of the past. Culture didn't need "civilizing," and the video store "facilitated a new brutalism," with Tarantino as its "most accomplished practitioner," according to Biskind.

But the whole mythos is a bit askew. Tarantino bears more of a resemblance to innovators such as Godard and Jean-Pierre Melville than to Roger Avary or Kevin Smith. The rough edges and pop icons that surround him are part of the mask he loves to wear. *Clerks* does not have the "esoteric structure" that Peter Wollen talks about; it builds its narrative on a playful and sad ennui that is powerful in itself but cannot bear multiple viewings; the jokes begin to flatten out and the characters grow more and more predictable until chaos turns to boredom. But the closer we scrutinize *Reservoir Dogs* and *Pulp Fiction,* the more we find. The structure of both films is hidden, almost malleable, and shifts each time we fall upon the characters and their turmoil.

Tarantino is quite cruel when it comes to Roger Avary, who contributed to the narrative of *Pulp Fiction* and shared an Academy Award for best screenplay: "Roger would be working at an advertising agency right now if my mother never met my father. If I never existed, Roger never would have directed one foot of film, ever. And if I hadn't written *Pulp Fiction,* he would never have won an Oscar."

But there's at least a *touch* of truth in what Tarantino says. He created a hurricane around him, a force field that swooped up video clerks and every other geek who wanted to make a film. There is no generation of video-clerk geniuses. There were several talented filmmakers who happened to roam around in shopping malls and gravitated toward the video store, in an age of shopping malls. But the video stores are growing barren in an age of DVDs. If Scorsese, Coppola, and Lucas prospered in the seventies, it wasn't because of any film school; it was because Hollywood was stuttering along and welcomed young directors with a vision and a tactile sense of cinema.

Tarantino grew up on the films of the seventies, absorbed them into his psyche as he absorbed everything else. He came along at a time when Hollywood was caught in a "square dance" mentality. And the *strangeness* of *Reservoir Dogs,* its originality, didn't work against him. Suddenly a "movie man" like Tarantino was marketable, an uncultivated video clerk, the South Bay Candide. But he was much more cultivated than Hollywood could ever have imagined, much more ambitious, much more certain of himself. And the video clerk had its own aura. "Now Video Archives is like LA's answer to the *Cahiers du Cinéma,*" Tarantino said in a *Rolling Stone* interview. "At William Morris they'll be telling agents: 'You've gotta check out the scene at the video store.' "

4.

He created his own scene, his own *noise,* moving about with his own fierce will. Film geeks had to "show a high regard for their own opinions . . . He with the most point of view wins. When I walk into a room, I always have the most point of view."

He was "a big, brawny, dangerous-looking dude. His hair's wild," writes one film critic. He dressed in black, wore a hoop earring, drove a Honda Civic, lived in a ratty apartment right in back of the store. He was the manager of Video Archives for a while, but even as manager he might not show up for work. He was fired several times, rehired, in that constant shuffle of clerks. Customers flocked to him and the films he adored. "He could sell you a date in the electric chair," says Lance Lawson.

He could be generous and very, very mean. "An only child, he doesn't share his toys," writes Jami Bernard. He would admit that he had "no sense of style"—about clothes, cars, or furniture. But that couldn't stop him from being a connoisseur of junk food, comic books, and board games. A director who makes a false movie and sins badly in a film "should go to movie jail" in Tarantino's universe, which consists of a giant Monopoly board.

As Steve Buscemi said about him, Tarantino has remained that child, alone in his room, with a giant TV as his friend, a kind of umbilical cord that comforts him. Critics have chided Tarantino for his creation of a "parallel universe" that seems utterly removed from the concerns of thinking, feeling, breathing adults. And they blame this on his absorption in the junk food of popular culture, like some prepubescent character mired in all sorts of artifice and paraphernalia—Yoo-hoo,

John Traviolta dolls, and brain-dead television serials—rather than in the romance of being alive. But Tarantino is very much alive, and his "parallel universe" resembles that of another prepubescent character, a nineteenth-century mathematics tutor, Charles Lutwidge Dodgson, who never married, spent much of his time chaperoning and photographing little girls, rarely strayed from his tower rooms at Christ College, and wrote two children's books, *Alice's Adventures in Wonderland* (1865) and *Through the Looking Glass* (1872), under the name of Lewis Carroll. Dodgson had a "studentship" at Oxford, where he could study whatever he wished so long as he remained unmarried, like a grown-up child. He performed magic tricks as a little boy and had a lifelong habit of collecting music boxes and mechanical toys. "Everything for Carroll pointed to disaster in his personal life. He was almost the case-book maladjusted neurotic," writes critic Peter Coveney; a "stammering, awkward, spinsterlike don, imprisoned within Christ's College, Oxford, from the age of nineteen till his death . . . Children were, he confessed, three fourths of his life." The beautiful and celebrated actress Ellen Terry, who was one of his adult friends, remarked: "He was as fond of me as he could be of anyone over the age of ten."

One of the mysterious charms of the *Alice* books is that they are like the conjuring act of a brutal and intelligent child. Carroll *becomes* Alice, a "fabulous monster" who is seven in the first book and six months older in the second. He assumes all her properties, as if he were a kind of literary cross-dresser. Some of those who observed him as he grew older, declared that "his face became girlish, and that he assumed the embarrassed mannerism of a little girl."

Whether this is one more myth or not, Dodgson-Carroll was obsessed with childhood, "when Sin and Sorrow are but names—empty words signifying nothing."

In the first *Alice* book, we meet the Queen of Hearts, a savage lady who has her own savage song: "Off with their heads!" Carroll called her the "embodiment of ungovernable passion—a blind and aimless fury." But critic and poet William Empson shrewdly observes that "the Queen of Hearts is a symbol of 'uncontrolled animal passion' seen through the clear but blank eyes of sexlessness" (or at least the illusion of sexlessness, since Alice's own cannibalistic wants are profoundly sexual). But Empson's words could also describe the gargoyles of *Reservoir Dogs* and *Pulp Fiction,* who keep barking about sex but are never driven by any deep desire. Vincent Vega (John Travolta) goes out on a "date" with Mia Wallace (Uma Thurman), his boss's wife, but both of them enter the kingdom of Jack Rabbit Slim's, where sexuality turns into nostalgia. Butch (Bruce Willis) and his girlfriend, Fabienne (Maria de Medeiros) are utterly sexless, even when they make love.

The magic kingdoms that Lewis Carroll and Tarantino reveal are terrifying *and* hilarious places that cover up a void—the nothingness that surrounds all human monsters, the chicken scratch that hides the blankness of a page, the barking voices that make us forget the merciless and blinding whiteness of the screen. Carroll in both *Alice* books and Tarantino in his first two films reveal the fragility of our own little worlds by taking us deep into a "forest" called Wonderland or LA, where time and space whirl in front of our eyes, where gargoyles like Vincent die and come alive again, where a swollen egg like Humpty Dumpty can become a literary critic and unicorns can outsmart little girls. Both Carroll and Tarantino understand the ferocious power of "play"—pure play—that lets us sing in the dark and jump right into the bestiary of a child, a tableau that is much more alluring than the rules and habits that belong to our civilized selves.

CHAPTER TWO

Reservoir Dogs and the Ex-Hunchback of Notre Dame

1.

Certain critics and several of the Archives Dogs themselves like to think of Tarantino as a whirlwind who arrived out of nowhere, preordained for a fabulous success—all the maestro of Video Archives had to do was hop along some magic squares like Alice in Looking-Glass Land and crown himself king of Hollywood. The boy who wanted to be a star willed himself into one. But that's not how Tarantino reads the bumps and curves in his own career. He struggled as a screenwriter with a particular bent. He didn't want to be a hired gun in someone else's orbit. Tarantino claims he never "wrote things to sell. I wrote thinks to make. But I never had any success. It was a wasted life."

He began a film during his first years at Video Archives, called it *My Best Friend's Birthday,* worked on it with Roger Avary and other Archives Dogs and acquaintances from his acting classes. He poured whatever cash he had into the film, and was forever broke. He and Roger had their own powerful bond. They started out as competitors, suspicious of one another, but Roger soon realized that "we had the exact same tastes. It was kismet." The opening scene occurred in the control booth of K-Billy's radio station. Tarantino would salvage "K-Billy," use it again in *Reservoir Dogs,* where the station is "sort of this invisible character," or a haunted house that hovers over the action. "Me and Roger wrote all the commercials that went into the movie [*Reservoir Dogs*], traffic reports, editorials, everything."

But *My Best Friend's Birthday* couldn't seem to complete itself, despite Tarantino's guerrilla tactics. The energy drained out of him, and the film ended up as "guitar picks," yet it was a rather atypical guitar. The idea for the film had come from Craig Hamann, who'd been in his acting classes with James Best. Tarantino and Hamann co-wrote the final script. The film was meant to *reveal* their talent as actors and serve as a kind of calling card. Tarantino plays Clarence Pool, a disc jockey at "K-Billy." He looks like a vampire who loves to wear a gypsy earring and masquerade as Elvis. His opening riff tells how a Hollywood sitcom (*The Partridge Family*) saved him from suicide. Hamann plays Mickey, Clarence's best friend, who can't hold on to girlfriends or a job. Clarence hires a hooker for one night as Mickey's birthday present. But her pimp breaks in on them and Mickey ends up with nothing, as usual. Tarantino would pick at the bones of the film in *True Romance,* where another Clarence, who's also an

Elvis man, runs away with Alabama, a hooker who was lent to him for one night. Allen Garfield also appears in *My Best Friend's Birthday,* where he tells Clarence that "Marlon Brando was a great actor," but that Elvis (as an actor) "was a lost cause." Tarantino could have cannibalized his own acting classes in this scene, his own séances, his own arguments, with Allen Garfield. The entire film feels like a rehearsal for something else, a laboratory for Tarantino's future projects. The film bathes in its own hysteria; the lighting is poor; the sound seems to be coming from some muffled microphone, but *My Best Friend's Birthday* has a raw energy that Tarantino would rediscover in *Reservoir Dogs.*

The film hardly helped at all. He found a manager, Cathryn Jaymes, but he still couldn't find any work as an actor. He had "eight years of nothing," he said to Charlie Rose. He completed *True Romance* in 1987 while he was still at Video Archives, but couldn't get a single bite from *anyone* in Hollywood. The script would come back, "sometimes C.O.D.," with the cruelest of rejection letters, calling it the *dreck* of a madman.

Tarantino moved back in with his mother in 1989, after leaving Video Archives. He scratched out another script, *Natural Born Killers,* about a pair of homicidal maniacs, Mickey and Mallory Knox, who become media stars in media-mad America. Tarantino wanted the role of Mickey for himself in a film he meant to produce. He seemed to have a fondness for deranged killers in a trailer-trash culture. Mickey Knox is an amalgam of Mickey Rourke and Tarantino's Knoxville, Tennessee.

Rourke is the bad boy of American cinema; he grew up in one of the poorest hovels of Miami, became an amateur boxer, ran off to New York to study acting, and lived "underground" as a parking lot attendant, a pretzel vendor, and a Good Humor man. He would get into fights with directors whenever he appeared in an off-off-Broadway production. In Hollywood by 1979, he was cast as a sympathetic, soft-voiced arsonist and bombmaker in *Body Heat* (1981). He would become a star in Oliver Stone's *Year of the Dragon* (1985) and Allan Parker's *Angel Heart* (1987), where he plays a private detective whose psyche unravels while he runs after a killer who turns out to be himself. He's the ultimate amnesiac on screen, dangerous, unpredictable, and childlike. Tarantino must have seen a bit of himself in Mickey Rourke, one of his *and* Connie's favorite actors. But Rourke's stardom didn't last very long. He began to self-destruct—fighting, drinking, using drugs—and he dropped out of sight, resurfacing in Miami as a professional boxer under the name of Marielito . . . until *Sin City* (2005) where he plays Marv, a sad-eyed brute as close to Mickey Rourke as any character can get.

Tarantino had no more luck with *Natural Born Killers* than he did with *True Romance*. He began to see himself as the ultimate outsider who would have to work as a guerrilla on a guerrilla production beyond the Hollywood mainstream. He wrote *Reservoir Dogs* in three and a half weeks during October 1990. He would add the film within the film—Mr. Orange's riff about the cops and the German shepherd—in a second draft. He happened to meet a young producer, Lawrence Bender, who was as much of an outcast as he was. "We were both very broke at the time," according to Bender. "You know, he didn't have a car, so he couldn't drive over to my place. I didn't have money, so I wasn't paying for xeroxes. So I came over to his place and I read the script. And obviously I flipped over it. . . . And I said, 'Look, you gotta give me some time. I think I can raise some real money for this movie.' "

But Tarantino, who had been burnt before by Hollywood producers with their riffs about raising money, would only give him two months. And it's here that the myth of the magical producer begins, a man with "the delicate features of a dancer and the cold ambition of a hit man," as Jami Bernard calls Lawrence Bender. But he's much less mythical than that. Bender was born in the Bronx, moved to South Jersey, and studied civil engineering at the University of Maine, because his grandfather was a civil engineer. But he didn't have a clue about his own calling. "I was going to become a potter. I almost quit college to go to chef's school."

He became a dancer because his girlfriend studied dance.

He had a scholarship with the Louis Falco dance company, and was a flamenco dancer for a little while until he injured his knees and back. He waited on tables and studied acting with Sandra Seacat, whose other pupils were Jessica Lange and Mickey Rourke.

He went out to Hollywood, couldn't find any work as an actor, and stumbled into producing. He would have continued to stumble if it hadn't been for Harvey Keitel, who fell upon the script of *Reservoir Dogs* through a friend of his, the divorced wife of an actor with whom Lawrence had been taking an occasional class. Without this circuitous route *Reservoir Dogs* might never have been made, or would have ended up another half-completed home movie, like *My Best Friend's Birthday*.

Keitel loved the script. "All of a sudden," said Tarantino, he and Lawrence Bender "weren't just a couple of kids anymore, with a script, just like everyone else had. We actually had Harvey Keitel." Keitel was as much a gypsy as Bender and Tarantino. Born in Brooklyn in 1941, he joined the Marines at seventeen, was sent to Beirut, became a court reporter, studied with Lee Strasberg at the Actors Studio, performed at coffeehouses, and appeared in Martin Scorsese's first film, *Who's That Knocking at My Door?* (1968).

He's also had his own strange, peripatetic career as a character actor who could submerge himself in a role with a kind of intensity that few other actors can equal, but his "quietness" on screen often rendered him less visible than the actors and actresses around him. Scorsese's *Mean Streets* (1973) should have made him a star, but the camera fell in love with Robert De Niro's performance as the dimwitted Johnny Boy with the electric walk, and Keitel remained in the background, almost as De Niro's straight man. He should have been the star of Francis Ford Coppola's *Apocalypse Now* (1979), where he was supposed to play Captain Willard, a soldier-assassin who travels down the Mekong to kill a renegade colonel (Marlon Brando) in Cambodia. Shot in the Philippines, the film was beset with all sort of problems, such as a typhoon and Coppola's megalomania, and Keitel walked away from the project, because he couldn't get along with Coppola.

He wandered through Europe for a while, played Tom Paine in *La Nuit de Varennes* (1982) and Pontius Pilate in *The Inquiry* (1987); he was Judas in Scorsese's adaptation of Nikos Kazantzakis's *Last Temptation of Christ* (1988). But Keitel is much too contemporary for the words he had to mouth and the costumes he had to wear; his power on screen is to reveal *himself* in whatever role he has to play. As Sam Fuller complained to Tarantino about *Reservoir Dogs*: "You make a movie for idiots. Too much gibble-gabble! Too much talk. Harvey Keitel! He's not an actor. He's a planet!" Fuller's films are full of gibble-gabble. He brings his own sense of animation to the dialogue he writes, a kind of snarling repartee that is one of the real delights of *Pickup on South Street* (1953) and *Shock Corridor* (1963). Tarantino needed a planetary force like Harvey Keitel to hold the narrative together, to soften the strangeness of *Reservoir Dogs*, to make the other actors more credible. And he needed Keitel's presence to finance the film.

In the prescribed world of independent filmmaking, Keitel was indeed a planet and much, much more—one of Scorsese's fetish actors who pops up in five of his films. And Keitel lent his weight and legitimacy to a pair of geeks who couldn't afford a Xerox machine. But the film also served Keitel's own interests, his desire to become a "guerrilla" who didn't have to wait for approval from Paramount or Fox. He regretted not having made his own films when he started out as an actor. "We were struggling to make a living ourselves, to get work, to get agents, the whole thing." And he saw in Tarantino a surrogate, someone who had the raw courage to break out and begin. Keitel flew the geeks to New York out of his own pocket to help with auditions. He put them up at the Mayflower; Tarantino fed on caviar for the first time in his life (at the Russian Tea Room). It was in New York that they found Steve Buscemi, a slightly smaller planet in the independent film world; quirky, irascible, he fit within a landscape of foulmouthed hoods and could range into Tarantino's rabbit hole, with Keitel beside him.

Tarantino was one of eight applicants (out of a thousand) accepted at Robert Redford's Sundance Film Institute to work on their projects at the Filmmakers Lab in June 1991. At Sundance, Tarantino rehearsed and shot on video the bathroom scene in *Reservoir Dogs*, where Mr. White and Mr. Pink dissect the details of their botched robbery. Buscemi had come to the lab with Tarantino, and he played Mr. Pink, while Tarantino himself was Mr. White. Terry Gilliam, one of the directors who served as an advisor while Tarantino was in residence, liked the closed-in atmosphere of the scene, encouraged Tarantino, told him that putting a film in one room was as close as he could get to "pure cinema."

Tarantino was lucky to have Gilliam around. Gilliam was a "purist" who understood Tarantino's sense of architecture, of sculpting in film, of pushing against boundaries; his own films, such as *Brazil* (1985) and *The Fisher King* (1991), were all about rabbit holes, about redefining "possible" and "impossible."

With the financing in place ($1.3 million) and the film completely cast, principal photography would begin on July 29, 1961, and last five weeks. "I didn't use storyboards because I can't draw, and I didn't like the idea of someone else drawing them because they wouldn't get the framing right. But I can write, so I did extensive shots, where I just describe everything." Yet one almost feels that Tarantino had a storyboard inside his head, that like Terry Gilliam, or Lewis Carroll, he could float in his own mirror world from abstraction to abstraction and take all of us along on the ride.

2.

We open in the dark. Tarantino's voice leaps out at us. He's delivering one of his riffs, a spiel from acting class about Madonna's "Like a Virgin." "The whole song is a metaphor for big dick." It doesn't have the sadness of Dennis Hopper's riff in *True Romance* or the comic pull of Christopher Walken's in *Pulp Fiction*. It *belongs* in an acting class. It's a false start. The camera takes a complete turn around a table of men, a shot Tarantino is quite proud of, but it creates confusion, together with the rub of his voice as he recites "dick, dick, dick, dick . . ."

But the camera quiets down soon as we get to Harvey Keitel. He steals Lawrence Tierney's address book. It's Tierney who's the marvel of this scene, Tierney the delinquent actor who played John Dillinger in 1945, who was the most *noir* actor of all time, the star of *Born to Kill* and *The Devil Thumbs a Ride*– handsome, brutal, without a touch of pity. He seemed to fade without the offices of film noir, would get into drunken brawls, as if he could no longer tell the difference between playing Dillinger and the Devil on or off the screen. He surfaced in 1973, after being stabbed in a Manhattan bar . . .

Tarantino first met him in the middle of a party at the Actors Studio. "He's an older guy, and had only so much to give in terms of stamina. He's a good guy, but he can slow you up 30 percent. He's alternately a teddy bear and a grizzly bear. . . . Do you remember his 1947 film, *The Devil Thumbs a Ride*? That could almost be entitled *The Lawrence Tierney Story.*"

And the key to his performance is that he is a teddy bear *and* a grizzly bear in the same instant. He breaks into Tarantino's Madonna riff with his rough, gravelly voice. "Toby . . . who the fuck is Toby?" It's a delicious counterpoint to Tarantino's polemics as Mr. Brown. He finds an old address book "in a jacket I ain't worn in a coon's age," and he goes through the inventory of names. "Toby what? What the fuck was her last name?"

It undercuts Brown's pretentiousness as a purveyor of pop culture, like some hoodlum having an hysterical fit—a "virgin" actor who's trying to trick the camera with talk. But Keitel takes over in his tug-of-war with Tierney over the address book. And Steve Buscemi as Mr. Pink delivers his own spiel about tipping. "I don't tip because society says I gotta tip . . ." The hysteria is gone. We believe in Buscemi as we never believe in Mr. Brown . . . or in novelist Eddie Bunker, who plays Mr. Blue without that *emphasis* an actor needs, words traveling through a persona. If Brown and Blue disappear from the film, it's not because they are killed; it's because their presence was never really felt on screen. We can't mourn those we haven't missed. Their faces and voices do not rivet us; our eyes wander while they speak . . .

We're at a diner. The Dogs are having breakfast. We haven't a clue about why they are there. Six of them sit in black suits and thin black ties. The other two, Joe Cabot (Lawrence Tierney) and his son, Nice Guy Eddie (Chris Penn) are wearing much more casual clothes. There are no guns or knives on the table, and Mr. Blonde (Michael Madsen), who will become a homicidal maniac as we move deeper into the film, seems a soft and sensitive knight who defends Madonna against Tarantino's diatribe. " 'Like a Virgin,' " he says, "[is] about a girl who is very vulnerable and she's been fucked over a few times."

The Dogs could be disc jockeys. "Have you guys been listening to K-Billy's Super Sounds of the Seventies Weekend?" Nice Guy Eddie asks.

"Yeah, it's fuckin' great, isn't it," says Mr. Pink.

K-Billy will haunt the film like a leitmotiv we can't get away from. And we're all stuck in the middle of the same weekend, with K-Billy and the Dogs, who are never really identified except for Joe and Mr. Pink. Otherwise they're nameless nobodies in peculiar attire.

Pink steals the scene with a riff that Tarantino must have swiped from his acting classes, but it's Steve Buscemi who's delivering the lines; like any good film actor, he knows when to hide and when to reveal himself. He has his own "aura" on the screen. He soothes us as the camera hovers around his face. We can locate ourselves in relation to him. *His* riff anchors us. Tarantino's friends and accomplices from his Video Archives days remember him as a notorious non-tipper, and it's Tarantino's absurd passion and philosophy of non-tipping that animates Mr. Pink and drives the narrative.

When the Dogs defend waitresses who count on tips to stay alive, Mr. Pink rubs two of his fingers together. "Do you know what this is? It's the world's smallest violin, playing just for the waitresses."

But Joe obliges him to leave a tip, and he tells the Dogs, "Okay ramblers, let's get rambling." And they do. As we fade to black, we hear a voice announce that K-Billy's Super Sounds of the Seventies "just keeps on truckin'." The Dogs do a kind of slow-motion waltz outside the restaurant to one of K-Billy's Super Sounds—"Little Green Bag," and now we're in the midst of the title sequence. And for the first time all eight men are identified as "Reservoir Dogs," though they've never once discussed their heist.

We fade to black again, hear a man whine, "I'm gonna die," and open onto a blood-soaked car, with Harvey Keitel driving and clutching the hands of Tim Roth, who's writhing on the backseat, writhing in his own blood. He's been shot in the stomach. It's right after a botched robbery, but we don't know that. We're a little lost in the confined space, and the scene itself feels stagy, as if we're not able to enter that car with the two Dogs; it's *film* blood, after all, much too red, and the car doesn't rock with a chaos that would take us outside movie time. It reminds us of a prop. We're watching two men perform in a static arena. We resist that cutaway car and the two Dogs, want to run from them and the film.

But the tempo changes the moment they crash through the door of a warehouse where all the Dogs are supposed to rendezvous after the robbery; the film begins to breathe. And it's odd that the warehouse doesn't make us claustrophobic, doesn't seal us inside, but becomes its own universe, and we never want to leave. We've come to Tarantino's Wonderland, where stories move with the rhythm of a merciless clock.

Pink arrives, and there's no more random chatter. "Was that a fucking set-up or what?"

He's the shrewdest and most professional of the Dogs. He realizes that chance had little to do with what went wrong. ". . . where did all those cops come from, huh? One minute they're not there, the next minute they're there."

But the backstory isn't important. What's important is Tarantino's sudden control of the camera, a relentless control. We don't have complete turns around a table, with the camera leaving dead zones in its wake. We don't have Tarantino ranting "dick, dick, dick, dick." We have close-up after close-up—of White, Orange, and Pink—as the camera sculpts with an intimacy, a hard but loving edge. We have faces eating up the screen, faces that are more potent than any twists in the narrative, faces that defy the cinematic machine.

3.

The Dogs are in need of a locale, their own crazy kennel, where they can hide. In *Les Cahiers du Cinéma,* Camille Nevers speaks of "the suffocating, claustrophobic space of the film." And Larissa MacFarquhar, in her *New Yorker* profile of Tarantino, writes: "To keep the budget small, he set the movie in one location, a warehouse, and made a virtue of that necessity by creating the sort of intense claustrophobia and paranoia that can arise only when characters with reasons to distrust one another are penned up and unable to leave." What MacFarquhar says is true in theory: the warehouse is enclosed; the Dogs are penned up and suspicious of one another (except for White's touching but dumb devotion to Orange, who was put there to betray them all, even with the bullet in his belly). But there's nothing claustrophobic about the way Tarantino films the warehouse; it feels like some infinity against the constant close-ups of the Dogs themselves, as if the Dogs had left whatever danger befell them in the void outside. The cops are waiting for Joe Cabot (Tierney) to appear, so they can pounce as soon as the Dogs leave the warehouse.

When the film was shown at Sundance in June 1992, the

festival's program notes described *Reservoir Dogs* as "Jim Thompson meets Samuel Beckett." And it's a rather appropriate tag: the vicious pulp art of Thompson mingled with the profound isolation of Beckett, with Beckett's own sense of infinity in the enclosed wildlands of *Waiting for Godot* (1954), where the only prop is a tree.

Tarantino himself has called *Reservoir Dogs* the pulp novel he would never write. But it's a "pulp novel" with his own wild form and all the sadness of foulmouthed men who can never really articulate their own hunger. They are stranded in the space that Tarantino has found for them, with murder being the only language they can express; aggression is their own peculiar form of tenderness.

And it's fitting that the warehouse Tarantino chose was a former house of the dead, an abandoned mortuary at Figueroa and 59th, in the Highland Park section of *old* LA, far from all the glitz (the building would disappear in an earthquake). Tarantino didn't bother to "redress" the mortuary; coffins stand upended like strange sarcophagi in sleeves; Mr. Blonde sips his soft drink while sitting on a hearse disguised with a plastic cover. And White and Pink duck into an embalming room to discuss Orange's fate; we can even recognize the embalming fluids.

The mortuary was infested with rats, and set decorator Sandy Reynolds-Wasco had to clean up Orange's "pool of blood" every day, or the rats wouldn't have left them alone. The warehouse was insufferably hot, and Orange kept sticking to his own fake blood. "It's a syrup and it dries under the lights, so you're actually stuck to the floor at some points," Tim Roth recalls. Orange did have the look of a trapped spider as he lay dying.

There was one other marvelous space, a graffiti-mad wall in downtown LA, where Freddy Newendyke rehearses his riff in front of his acting coach, Holdaway, the undercover cop in the green cap. The wall once belonged to a subway exit of an older, abandoned underground.

"It's under a freeway, a flyover thing," according to Roth. "It's an incredible place, a big outdoor auditorium and there's a stage. At the side of the stage there's two doors and behind the doors live two tramps. All weekend they'd come and stick their heads out while we were filming. They'd been living there for years and neither of them likes each other, but they're neighbors and they live this far apart [he holds his hands a couple of feet away from each other] and they really don't like each other, but it's amazing."

These two tramps could have walked right out of *Waiting for Godot*, or moved into Tarantino's film as additional Dogs . . .

The cruelest moment of the film belongs to Mr. Blonde, the "trigger-happy madman" who shot everyone in sight after the alarm went off at the robbery. Pink doesn't believe that Mr. Blonde could be the rat who betrayed them. "He's too fuckin' homicidal to be workin' with the cops."

Blonde has captured a cop, kept him in the trunk of his car as some kind of trophy. The cop's name is Marvin Nash. Blonde shows him off to Mr. White and Mr. Pink. *"The three crooks share a frightening laugh,"* Tarantino tells us.

We meet Marvin again inside the warehouse. The Dogs have knocked the crap out of him, taped him to a chair. White and Pink leave with Nice Guy Eddie, and Blonde is left to "babysit" Orange and the cop.

"Alone at last," Blonde says. He pulls a razor out of his boot, pretends to shave himself. He wears suspenders and a thin black tie, a holster tucked under his left arm. He could be a maniacal rockabilly, an Elvis clone practicing for a bloodbath. Blonde disturbs us because there's nothing baroque about him—he's no Freddy Krueger, with a sinister scarred face. The mise-en-scène won't allow us to distance ourselves from Michael Madsen and the cop he mutilates. The camera seduces us, pulls us in with its own intimacy, as if Tarantino were plotting a seduction scene. Blonde seems to coo at the cop with a crazy, lulling voice. "I don't really give a good fuck what you know or don't know. But I'm gonna torture you anyway . . . regardless. Not to get information, but it's amusing to me to torture a cop."

He turns on the radio to K-Billy's Super Sounds of the Seventies. He does his own little snake dance to Stealer's Wheel's rendering of "Stuck in the Middle with You," the razor in his fist. The razor that lashes out at Marvin is also lashing at us. We can't avoid our own mutilation.

He cuts off Marvin's ear, bathes him in gasoline, and is about to set him on fire, when Orange wakes from the dead to shoot Mr. Blonde.

Ella Taylor, like a good many other critics, is appalled by what happens to Marvin. "The torture scene infuriates me because it has no point other than to show off its technique, and to jump-start our adrenaline." But the scene is not as gratuitous as Ella Taylor thinks.

"The cinema isn't intruding in that scene," Tarantino told Ella Taylor. "You are stuck there, and the cinema isn't going to help you out. Every minute for that cop is a minute for you." Or as he said to Larissa MacFarquhar: "I like fucking with your emotions, and I like it when it's done to me. That's my thing . . . The audience and the director, it's an S & M relationship, and the audience is the M." Yet it's not quite as simple as that. Tarantino may be a magician and his own kind of "dominatrix." He may even purr at us: "You're supposed to laugh until I stop you laughing," and believe that "Stuck in the Middle with You" puts us all in a particular mood. "[Y]ou're tapping your toe and you're enjoying Michael

Madsen doing his dance and then, *voom*, it's too late, you're a co-conspirator."

But we aren't tapping our toes. We're hypnotized, caught in Madsen's spell, and it's not Tarantino who's the real conjurer here, while he monkeys with our emotions. It's Michael Madsen. And it's not so much the contrast between him and the song he dances to, though Tarantino would have us believe it is. "People have told me that whenever they hear that song from hereon in they're gonna just see Michael Madsen doing his dance."

Nor is it the *naturalness* of Madsen's performance. "That's what Mr. Blonde would *do* when left alone," Tarantino tells us. *Torture a cop.* But the horror of the scene doesn't so much depend on our witnessing Marvin's mutilation as it does on our fear that Madsen really is Mr. Blonde, that the role is bringing out some sort of psychosis in him, and that this psychosis might inhabit our own skin, or at least mine, if not Ella Taylor's.

I can only recall two other performances that gave me such a chill—Jack Palance as the gunman with gloves and a mask-like face in George Stevens' *Shane* (1953) and Richard Widmark as the homicidal maniac with the hyena laugh in Henry Hathaway's *Kiss of Death* (1947). I might also include Robert Mitchum as the crazed preacher in Charles Laughton's *Night of the Hunter* (1955). Madsen resembles Mitchum; both of them have the same sleepy eyes and quiet look of menace. But Mitchum was already a star when he made *Night of the Hunter*, a star who can glide from role to role. And my memory of him as a likable grunt in William Wellman's *Story of G.I. Joe* (1945), or as the cowboy who rides on a raft with Marilyn Monroe in Otto Preminger's *River of No Return* (1954), eats into whatever menace he might have in any other film. But Madsen isn't encumbered by his own history. He hardly had one. He may have been in films before *Reservoir Dogs* (he's Susan Sarandon's boyfriend in Ridley Scott's *Thelma and Louise*), but he seems to blend right into the background as one more invisible man who keeps the stars company while they perform their own little bag of tricks.

And like some ingenious animal trainer, Tarantino reveals him to us. This is one of his great strengths as a director. He has an uncanny wisdom in picking his cast: he will weld an actor or actress to a role that will define them *forever*, or redefine them, as he did with John Travolta in *Pulp Fiction*, Pam Grier and Robert Foster in *Jackie Brown*, or Lucy Liu as the queen of the yakuza with a girlish voice in *Kill Bill Vol. 1*.

But we also have to consider the *accident* of performance and of the film itself. "I'm trying to wipe out every movie I ever wanted to make in the first one," he told Ella Taylor, as if he were looking back upon *Reservoir Dogs* as some instrument he was able to perfect and control. But films are about

chaos, about a little army of men and women—actors, techni-
cians, producers and such—coming together to find a form, to
dig about half-blind in a morass of detail. And the director
loves to pretend he's the kingpin. He (or she) can instigate,
seduce, cajole, but the film becomes some strange animal that
falls asleep (as most films do) or breathes its own fire. Tarantino provoked the brilliance of *Reservoir Dogs*, but the film
shaped him and his own little army more than he could ever
have imagined, and he was able to dance within its chaos, just
as "Blondie" danced.

Harvey Weinstein of Miramax (the film's distributor), aka
"Harvey Scissorhands," wanted to rid the film of Marvin's
mutilated ear. "Without this scene, you have a mainstream
film," he told Tarantino. "Without that scene, I could open this
film in three hundred theaters. As opposed to one! Thirty seconds would change the movie in the American marketplace."

But Tarantino resisted Weinstein's arguments, and he was
right to resist. *Reservoir Dogs* couldn't have opened "wide,"
with or without the torture scene. It wasn't *Pretty Woman*, he
told Harvey Scissorhands. And without the torture scene,
Reservoir Dogs would probably have dropped into oblivion as
one more arthouse film. "Blondie's" dance had mesmerized
audiences, whether they sat with their eyes shut or rushed out
of the cineplex to avoid Madsen's razor.

Tarantino is a bit disingenuous about the razor itself. "I try to explain to people that I didn't sit down and say, 'OK, I'm gonna write this really bitchin' torture scene.' When Mr. Blonde reached into his boot and pulled out a straight razor, I didn't know he had a straight razor in his boot. I was surprised. That happens all the time when I'm writing. I equate it to acting."

"Blondie's" dance is meaningless without the razor. We watch him shuffle back and forth with razor in hand. As he lunges, he seems to be challenging the whole cinematic machine, attacking the cop, ourselves, and the screen, as if he could tear a hole in it and leave us all wandering in some void. And this is what is so frightening. We've entered our own heart of darkness, but it would never have happened if Madsen didn't overpower us with the possibility of his own evil. No performance, no matter how nuanced or skilled, could rock us in the same way.

Madsen isn't a murderer, and supposedly he grew upset when Marvin tells him: "Please don't burn me . . . I got a little kid at home" (the lines were improvised, weren't in the actual script), but this isn't what we get on screen. There's a calmness and a coldness we've seldom encountered. Dennis Hopper is almost as evil in David Lynch's *Blue Velvet* (1986), where he plays a brutal drug dealer with a little breathing mask, but we can feel Hopper's pain, his hunger for Isabella Rossellini, and Mr. Blonde has no hunger other than to inflict pain. His dance is decidedly sexual. But it isn't Marvin who arouses him; it's the dream of destruction. "Was that as good for you as it was for me?" he asks, after jumping onto Marvin's lap and lopping off his ear. The camera pulls away from the scene of the crime; we're only allowed to see the warehouse. Then Mr. Blonde enters the frame and dances away with the cop's bloody ear. Never mind that it's a prosthetic device: the ear seems real enough. In his glee, Mr. Blonde talks to the ear as if it were a microphone. "Hey, what's goin' on?" he asks.

Much of the dialogue is improvised. The scene, as Tarantino had written it, is quite spare. But Madsen's demented dialogue goes right along with his demented dance. It's hard to imagine anyone else playing "Blondie," and neither can Madsen himself. "For the rest of my life, I'm going to be known as Mr. Blonde, the guy from the garage scene in *Reservoir Dogs.*"

Madsen had used his own car in the film, a '65 yellow Cadillac, which he sent to his sister's garage in Wisconsin, because he couldn't bring himself to sell the "Dogs Car." The film had fetishized Madsen, and should have carried him much further along in his career. He was offered the role of Vincent Vega in *Pulp Fiction* (Mr. Blonde is actually Vic Vega, Vincent's brother), but he turned it down to act in Lawrence Kasden's western, *Wyatt Earp* (1994)—a big, big mistake. "It was like three hours of nausea," he told Sanjiv Bhattacharya. Had he appeared in *Pulp Fiction*, he would have been Mr.

Blonde whether his name was Vic or Vince. And instead of a potbellied, comical John Travolta, we would have had "Blondie" as Samuel L. Jackson's killer sidekick. The film might have had a spookier edge, but how will we ever know?

Madsen was born in Chicago in 1958, and was raised by his father, a fireman. He sat in juvenile jail a couple of times for being a burglar, a brawler, and a car thief. He would work as a hospital orderly and might have remained there if he hadn't joined Chicago's Steppenwolf Theatre and studied with John Malkovich. Madsen's sense of the void may have come from Malkovich himself, an actor with his own quiet menace and a rage that seems to live under some hairline trigger inside himself. But Madsen's own isolation seems outside any acting class. One can sense this in the poetry he loves to scribble on "[h]otel napkins, bar bills, beer mats. I wrote a poem on my leg once, on the skin." In one of them, "Tuesday," he talks about being lost, alone, and suicidal, a freak admired by other freaks because he plays the freak . . .

4.

*R*eservoir Dogs had its own odd trajectory. It was the most talked about film at the Sundance Festival, where it had its first public screening. "It was completely wild," recalls Tim Roth. "They were selling tickets on the buses for $100 apiece," but it still didn't win any prize. Harvey Scissorhands took the film to Cannes, where it was displayed like some stepchild—a reservoir dog that wasn't allowed to compete for the Palme d'Or. But the French fell in love with the film, saw its originality, and adopted Tarantino, and that's when he began to play . . . Quentin Tarantino. He did his first interviews "like an actor would do a scene."

He was on the road with *Reservoir Dogs* for almost an entire year. "And the only reason anybody knows who I am is because I did a thousand interviews. I went to Spain, I went to Brazil, I did *all* the interviews." Yet interviews would have meant nothing without the appeal of the film, particularly to younger audiences. Harvey Scissorhands opened the film in New York and LA in October '92, limiting it to twenty-six screens. *Dogs* took in less than three million dollars "despite a hurricane of press," but the film did earn back its cost in ten weeks. And it was a monster hit in England, where it earned twice as much as it did in America. Tarantino became an instant idol and was mobbed wherever he went. He traveled from festival to festival with the film, Miramax right behind him.

Tim Roth recognized the shrewdness of Harvey Scissorhands. Miramax marketed Tarantino rather than the film or its cast. "What they did was put a machine around the movie very early because they knew they had something different."

The strategy paid off. *Reservoir Dogs* was an enormous

success at the video store, with its shopping mall culture and its anarchic urban audiences that could see themselves as genuine Dogs, though they couldn't have come up with a real definition of what a Reservoir Dog was.

People would stop Lawrence Tierney and ask him about the title. "Well, as you know," Tierney told a foreign journalist, "Reservoir Dogs is a very famous expression in America . . . for . . . dogs . . . who . . . hang around a reservoir." Tarantino had been worried that some minor movie mogul might want to change the title when he had to pitch the film to investors. So he would say: " 'It's an expression used in French New Wave gangster films. It's an expression meaning 'rat.' It's in *Breathless,* its in *Bande à part.'* A total lie, but they believed it. They hadn't seen those movies."

One of the reasons he chose the title "was that it sounds like something in an Alain Delon movie of Jean-Pierre Melville, who very much influenced me. I could see Alain Delon in a black suit saying, 'I'm Mr. Blonde.' "

Melville and Delon were appropriate sources for the film *and* its title. Melville made crazy versions of American gangster films, as Tarantino himself said. *Le Samourai* (1967) would serve as a particular inspiration for *Reservoir Dogs.* Alain Delon plays Jeff Costello, a hit man who is caught up in his own whirlwind of silence. Like the Dogs, he wears a black suit and a thin black tie and lives in a big barren room that is its own complete world, like the warehouse. The sound that breaks his own silence comes from his companion, a parakeet who provides him with whatever language or company he needs. The Paris that Jeff inhabits is as forlorn and nondescript as Tarantino's LA. There's no Eiffel Tower in *Le Samourai*, just garages, the bedroom of a woman who's more of an "alibi" than a mistress, and a myriad of Metro stations.

Tarantino's Dogs don't have Delon's panache; but their constant chatter is as isolating as his silence. The police are everywhere in *Le Samourai*. But they can't penetrate Delon; they can only kill him, or rather, help Jeff kill himself. The police are far less visible in *Reservoir Dogs*, but they are also everywhere, and will end up killing or capturing whatever Dogs haven't killed each other.

Both Melville and Tarantino sculpt empty space. *Reservoir Dogs* and *Le Samourai* exist in some netherland where there are no "ordinary people," just hoodlums, cops, and the human debris that surrounds them. "To make a film, all you need is a girl and a gun," Godard once said. There are no "girls" in *Reservoir Dogs*. We eavesdrop upon a curious bachelors' club that yaps about Madonna, Pam Grier, "white bitches and black bitches," but it's essential to the film that the Dogs be *deprived* of women. They're forlorn—gargoyles without much substance—and any "girl," with or without a gun, would diminish these gargoyles, make them human, shove us back to the near side of the Looking Glass, into the mundane world of mortgages and child support, which the Dogs couldn't abide, since *they* are the children.

The marvel of *Reservoir Dogs* is that with all the chaos of filmmaking, the confusion of moving a little army about, Tarantino was able to find a sense of "deep structure" in his very first film. He loves to pose as a rockabilly with the gift of memorizing films like some idiot savant, or a gangster manqué willing to destroy anyone who crosses him. "I don't fight by Marquess of Queensberry rules. When I fight, I fight like I'm trying to kill you, because I assume you're trying to kill me." But the gangster manqué is also a film theorist.

With *Kill Bill* in mind, Peter Biskind writes that Tarantino "may have loved Godard . . . but Hong Kong was his Paris, chop-socky his New Wave." I don't agree. The strengths and weaknesses of *Kill Bill* have little to do with "chop-socky." Tarantino's films are about architecture, or its absence, about building sequence after sequence like a bridge in the dark (a bridge you can't see), about using the tactics and machinery of a novelist. "What I really wanted was to make a novel on the screen, with characters who enter and exit, who have their own story but who can appear anywhere." And that's why Orange, Blondie, and White have their own "chapters" in the film rather than flashbacks, which Tarantino dislikes, because a flashback bears the burden of its own psychology and signature, while "chapters" are only connective tissue.

Eddie Bunker, who was a thief and a bank robber before he began to write and act in films, didn't have much faith in the Dogs and their black suits. "I mean it was absurd. There were these guys going to pull this big robbery and they're sitting in a coffee shop all dressed alike and the waitress knows them and they're tipping her (or not, as the case may be). If they went and pulled this big million dollar robbery, she'd pick up the newspaper and say, 'Hey, I know these guys . . .' "

But Tarantino wasn't looking for verisimilitude. He's fond of quoting Godard: "There is no blood in *Pierrot le Fou*. There is only the color red." *His* hoodlums sit in coffee shops, Tarantino's own favorite pastime. And they wouldn't be Reservoir Dogs if they didn't wear identical black suits.

So he sculpts around a robbery, brings us into a warehouse that functions like an endless barn where the Dogs can sniff and play and ruin themselves. As he told Charlie Rose: "It's a heist film where you never see the heist. That's just my goofy way of doing it—if I were going to do a hunchback movie, the guy'd get . . . some operation at the beginning of the film. The guy used to be the Hunchback of Notre Dame."

And it's this wildness, this slant, that gives *Reservoir Dogs* such a distinct flavor. Tarantino carves his own "hunchback" tale in the middle of an ex-mortuary.

CHAPTER THREE

Son of a Preacher Man

1.

Tarantino seemed to have brought along his own electricity, or perhaps the electricity was in his scripts. He liked to boast that "[e]very film should be better than its scenario, which is only a project, a kind of rehearsal for the film." But he loved to play the fox. Asked about *Reservoir Dogs* at a press conference in 1997, he said: "The razzle-dazzle came in the script form, the structure." Actor Danny DeVito sensed this "razzle-dazzle," read the script before there ever was a film, and advised Stacey Sher, President of Jersey Films (his own production company) to make a deal with Tarantino or risk losing him in the wake of *Reservoir Dogs*. Tarantino was offered "nearly a million dollars" to write and direct his next film. Suddenly the ex-clerk at Video Archives had become a "player" in Hollywood, who decided that he didn't want to direct *True Romance* or *Natural Born Killers,* since they were "like old girlfriends." He went to Amsterdam to work on *Pulp Fiction,* lived without a telephone, hung out at hash bars such as Betty Boop, sat with a book by the canals, attended a Howard Hawks festival, bought movie posters, and like some kind of crazy sponge absorbed whatever was around him. "Even though the movie [*Pulp Fiction*] takes place in Los Angeles, I was taking in all this weird being-in-Europe-for-the-first-time stuff and that was finding its way into the script. So some genre story that I'd had for five years started becoming personal as I wrote it."

Vincent Vega (John Travolta), the potbellied hood with the long hair, has just come back from Amsterdam, and the conversation he has with his fellow hood, Jules Winnfield (Samuel L. Jackson), as they are on their way to work a bit of mayhem, sets the tone for the odd mix of the familiar and unfamiliar that defines much of *Pulp Fiction* and makes its characters memorable even though they arrive and depart without much history or fanfare. They are comic characters, no matter how murderous they become, and the horror of two hitmen and the blood that engulfs them is driven out by the force of the dialogue.

Jules and Vince are sitting in a car in the same black suits as the Reservoir Dogs; they are Dogs, but in another picture. According to film historian Dana Polan, "one of the subtexts of *Pulp Fiction* is *Reservoir Dogs*," as Tarantino himself has said in several interviews. But it's more than subtext; it's a fluidity, a visual and verbal signature—*dangerous* dialogue—that binds both films, gives them a wholeness and a texture that few other filmmakers ever find . . .

Vincent tells Jules about "the little differences" between Europe and America. "Well, you can walk into a movie theater and buy a beer. And I don't mean just, like, in no paper cup. I'm talking about a glass of beer. And in Paris, you can buy a beer at McDonald's. And, you know what they call a Quarter-Pounder with Cheese in Paris?"

Jules is bewildered. "They don't call it a Quarter-Pounder with Cheese?"

"No, man," says Vincent, "they got the metric system there, they wouldn't know what the fuck a Quarter-Pounder is . . . They call it a Royale with Cheese."

And this tiny country of measurements—a seismograph of cultural signs—destroys the notion that Tarantino is lost within a world of film, like some ostrich trapped in the dark. He's not an ostrich, even if some film critics believe he is. He presents himself as the ultimate "movie man," who will one day retire from directing films and head for Montana, or some other place "with good air," live to be a hundred, have his own little movie theater, and show whatever he wants. And says Larissa MacFarquhar, suckered in by his soliloquy, "the thirty years that Tarantino spends as a director will be only an interlude in the hundred years he will spend as a fan."

But the man who went to Amsterdam with his felt tip

pens was burning with ambition, and he could cut himself off from friends and accomplices and writing partners when he had to. He'd planned to work on *Pulp Fiction* with Roger Avary, a fellow refugee from Video Archives. Roger had written an earlier screenplay, *Pandemonium Reigns*, the story about a boxer who throws a fight, has a girlfriend who loves pie (like Tarantino and many of his characters), has to go back to his apartment to recapture his father's watch, encounters two hillbillies at a pawnshop, where he also meets a "gimp" and observes an act of anal intercourse, but in Roger's script everybody dies. And the centerpiece of the tale, Captain Koons's riff to little Butch about the watch, was Tarantino's. As he says about Roger's contribution: "There are a bunch of ideas that belong to him: the hillbillies, the pawnbroker. He had invented the watch, for example, but I had to make up the history of the watch. I also made Fabienne [the boxer's girlfriend] into a French woman."

Tarantino found himself in Amsterdam, in Paris, at Cannes, and on the road with *Reservoir Dogs,* while *Pulp Fiction* grew into a 500-page monster. He would cut away at the monster, without Roger around. "[I]n the course of time it just became my baby, and I didn't want to write it with him."

What had started out as a collection of stories, like an issue of *Black Mask* (the classic pulp fiction magazine), grew into

three complex tales with intertwining characters. And Tarantino bought out Roger's rights to the scenario. Roger was
bitter, but there was nothing he could do: Tarantino had the
lawyers and the momentum, and Roger couldn't get anything
produced on his own. "Quentin is a brilliant guy, and he is
brilliant in a lot of ways, and one of those is managing his
career."

Suddenly his career ran awry. He'd finished the script in
January '93, but Jersey Films, which had bankrolled Tarantino by having "a first-look agreement with TriStar" (part of
Columbia Pictures), was caught empty-handed when TriStar
"passed" on *Pulp Fiction,* bewildered by a script without conventional heroes and a conventional time frame. Tarantino
was philosophical about it. TriStar, he said, "paid me a lot of
money to look at the script," but none of the other majors
wanted to take it on.

Enter Miramax and Harvey Scissorhands with perfect
timing. Miramax had just been bought up by Disney, and
the king of independent distributors had broken into the
Hollywood castle and could finance films on his own (with
Disney money). "Miramax went into overdrive, a Beetle
with a Cadillac engine." And as luck would have it, Tarantino's fate and future were tied to the Weinsteins (Harvey
and his brother Bob).

Pulp Fiction was the first film financed by the *new* Miramax, which could now take "an $8 million chance." But it wasn't *such* a chance. The Weinsteins had already nursed Tarantino's career along; they were investing in the director as much as the film, packaging Tarantino as a kind of guru who could also bring in a lot of money. "Miramax is in the Quentin Tarantino business," Harvey Scissorhands liked to crow. He'd solved the riddle of Tarantino's magic. "Expect the unexpected. That's why people love him."

He and his brother were "the two slobs from Queens with their ragtag, anything-goes company in Tribeca." They were like "aliens from another dimension" in the "white-bread" world of Walt Disney. But Michael Eisner, Disney's chief executive, realized how profitable "the two slobs" could be. Harvey loved to paint himself as an ogre, or "an 800-pound gorilla," but Eisner knew how to handle gorillas. He lent Harvey a bigger and bigger cage.

The name Miramax was derived from the Weinsteins' own parents, Miriam and Max. They'd started out as promoters of rock concerts, and used the same tactics in promoting independent films. They had a mobster mentality, with Harvey as the baddest guy on the block. Born in '52, he was six feet tall, "300 pounds and counting . . . with eyes like olive pits staring out of a round, pasty face, neck like a fireplug, and hands as big as lambchops." He often went ballistic. "He tore phones out of walls and hurled them. He slammed doors and overturned tables. Almost anything in reach could become a weapon—ashtrays, books, and tapes, the framed family photographs sitting on his desk that he'd heave at some hapless executive and watch as they hit the wall, exploding in a shower of glass . . . It was theater—of cruelty." According to one former executive, this anger was purely "strategic." And brother Bob was involved in the same ordeal. "They were good and evil in one package," according to another source.

"If I didn't exist, they'd have to invent me—I'm the only interesting thing around," said Harvey Scissorhands, and Harvey wasn't wrong. He and Bob had been able to compete with the studios because they understood that a "small film" was really a big film waiting to be let out of its box. The Weinsteins had to get down and dirty, had to be rough. "In the studio world, you're imprisoned in a gilded cage. In the indie world, you're in a hole, which is darker, dirtier, and a lot smaller." And they thrived in their hole, made it expand with their commando tactics, with their own will; they spent money, politicked to win Academy awards, and began winning them and the Palme d'Or at Cannes. Two Miramax films, Jane Campion's *The Piano* and Chen Kaige's *Farewell, My Concubine* would share Cannes' top prize in 1993, a year after *Reservoir Dogs* was shown out of competition.

Harvey had a new pet in the house, behaved as if Tarantino was built right into the walls of Miramax. "He's working
class, we're working class." But Harvey couldn't test his
tantrums on Tarantino. The fits he threw and the walls he
broke got him nowhere. Daniel Day-Lewis was in his "stable"
of stars, and Harvey wanted him to play Vincent Vega. "And
when Harvey pushes for something, it registers on the
Richter scale." Daniel Day-Lewis had some clout at the box
office, and Travolta had none. The man whom Michael Eisner
had once called the biggest movie star on the planet was
drowning in one mediocre film after the next and had lost his
following and any belief in himself. He was coasting along,
one more millionaire actor who loved to fly his own planes,
until Tarantino "found" him.

And Tarantino is hard to resist. He spent twelve hours with
Travolta sitting over board games to *Grease, Saturday Night
Fever,* and *Welcome Back, Kotter* (the hit television series that
had launched Travolta and brought him out to Hollywood to
play Vinnie Barbarino, a loveable lightweight). But he
wouldn't butter up Travolta; he chided him for the poor
choices he'd made.

"I was kind of moved and hurt at the same time," Travolta
remembers. "He took me off guard . . . So I went home and
kinda stewed in my thoughts and realized that this guy
cared. He cares more about me than anyone has ever cared

about me professionally in my life . . . I meant something to him onscreen, the way as a kid Jimmy Cagney meant a lot to me."

Travolta wasn't delighted with the role of Vincent Vega at first. He didn't want to play a heroin addict who goes around killing people. "I wasn't sure that I could morally or ethically align myself with this kind of movie," he said. But Tarantino cooed at him and "helped me realize that he is portraying crime and drugs in a very unglamorous way."

As *unglamorous* as Uma Thurman, looking like some wayward angel who's come down from heaven to visit with us for a little while, or Travolta himself on a heroin high, inhabiting his very own dream street; drugs *and* crime are woven into the "tapestry" (as Tarantino calls the film), are essential to the comedy and the force of whatever narrative there is. Tarantino sang his song, and Travolta believed it. But Travolta was shrewd about one thing, the cadences he needed to sing his lines. "I think I was the only one who ever asked him [Tarantino] to rewrite. If I ran into a little area that I couldn't make work, I'd have him do it, and then he'd see that there was a word or something that wasn't quite right, and he'd rewrite it. The thing is he's a good actor, and he knows what he's doing." But Tarantino wasn't *acting* when he fended off Harvey Scissorhands over Daniel Day-Lewis. Behind his gangster talk was a gangster mentality. "One of the reasons I don't have a gun is, if I had a gun and a twelve-year-old kid broke into [my] house, I would kill him . . . There would be no holding you for the cops, no shooting to wound. I would empty the gun until you were dead. I feel that way about my art as well. I know that at the end of the day no one will mess with [my] movie to the point that I'm unhappy with it."

2.

Pulp Fiction leaves its mark from the opening scene; we don't have the nervousness of eight men around a table, with the camera moving in and out of obscurity while Tarantino adds to the hysteria with his talk about "dick, dick, dick, dick." We have two petty criminals sitting in a coffee shop, Honey Bunny (Amanda Plummer) and Pumpkin (Tim Roth). We catch them in the middle of a conversation. The camera never varies, never moves close, but seems to lock them in a kind of embrace. We could almost be watching a still life: Pumpkin and Honey Bunny seem part of the decor. They sit near a window, but the view is partially blocked by Venetian blinds. The territory within the frame is neutral, allowing us to concentrate not so much on Pumpkin and Honey Bunny themselves, but on what they tell us. We can't immediately locate them as criminals.

"You sound like a duck," Honey Bunny says, as Pumpkin is about to go into his riff. "Quack, quack, quack, quack, quack, quack, quack . . ."

They laugh; we can feel the warmth in their voices; a waitress with a round face bursts into the frame, smiles, and says, "Can I get anybody any more coffee?" And we have the first close-up of the film.

She doesn't really intrude; she's like a piece of decorative material with moving lips. And then we get back to our tableau, as Pumpkin discusses the risks of his milieu and métier. "Nobody ever robs restaurants, why not? Bars, liquor stores, gas stations, you get your head blown off stickin' up one of them. Restaurants, on the other hand, you catch with their pants down. They're not expecting to get robbed. Not as expecting, anyway."

Meanwhile, Pumpkin cries out to the waitress, *"Garçon. Coffee!"*

And the waitress intrudes upon the frame again, but only a tiny piece of her. "'Garçon' means boy," she says, correcting Pumpkin, as if she were some deus ex machina commenting on the action, but a deus ex machina who has little power to control.

Pumpkin reminds Honey Bunny that the last time they robbed a liquor store customers kept coming in and she "got the idea of takin' their wallets."

And like some little philosopher of crime, Pumpkin continues: "A lot of people come to restaurants."

"A lot of wallets," says Honey Bunny.

And they know what they're going to do next. The camera's own neutrality can end, and we have our first close-up of Pumpkin and Honey Bunny as they kiss and eat up the entire screen.

Pumpkin puts his .32 on the table; it looks like a puny thing. We worry about his welfare. "Everybody be cool, this is a robbery."

Honey Bunny has been soft and catlike, watching Pumpkin with an adorer's eyes. But the cuddly cat turns into a vixen as she clutches her own gun and waves it at the customers in the coffee shop. "Any of you fuckin' pricks move and I'll execute every motherfuckin' last one of you."

The soundtrack begins with its own crazy crescendo of "Misirlou" and we move right into the credits rolling on a black screen. Midway through the credits we can hear the static that accompanies the turning of a radio knob; someone has switched stations on us, and we jump into "Jungle Boogie," performed by Kool & The Gang, and Tarantino has given us all the clues we'll ever need. He's going to switch channels, take us on a roller-coaster ride, but not without giving us seat belts and a safety net. The camera will protect us, and so will Tarantino's sense of comedy.

Honey Bunny and Pumpkin are little murderous demons who could have stepped out of Lewis Carroll country and into the coffee shop. They are the first in a series of couples that wander through *Pulp Fiction,* and half the fun comes from Tarantino's odd finagling as the couples constantly shift: Vincent and Jules, Vincent and Mia, the boxer and Fabienne (Maria de Medeiros), the boxer and Marsellus (Ving Rhames) . . .

But the archetype of all these couples is Pumpkin and Honey Bunny, and Tarantino was persistent about who would play them. He wrote the parts with Amanda Plummer and Tim Roth in mind. "They are friends in real life, and when I ran into them one night at a party I was struck with a director's intuition: their size, their look, their energy, everything about them made me want to use them together in my film."

And he would allow no interference. In dealing with Mike Medavoy, the head of TriStar, Tarantino presented a cast list, with Tim Roth at the top of the list to play Pumpkin. "Tim Roth is a very fine actor," said Medavoy, "but Johnny Depp is also on your list. I would rather offer the part to Johnny Depp. And if he turns it down, we should go to Christian Slater."

Tarantino asked Medavoy what he'd always wanted to ask a movie mogul. "Do you actually think that Johnny Depp, in the role of Pumpkin, who's only in the last scene and the first scene, do you actually think that would mean a dollar's worth of difference at the box office?"

No, said Medavoy. "It wouldn't mean a dime, but it would make me feel better."

Tarantino had to maneuver around TriStar, Miramax, and other potential producers to guarantee his cast and give actors their own room to breathe. "Tarantino doesn't so much write his characters as hover over them, protecting their freedom of expression," says Ella Taylor. And the power of *Pulp Fiction*–its texture and its *teeth*–comes from Tarantino's ability to imagine an actor or actress within a role. He had to convince Uma Thurman over and over again to play Mia. She'd been frightened by the rawness of *Reservoir Dogs*, though she admired the movie. She read Tarantino's new script. "I found it rather terrifying. But I was just overwhelmed by his incredible energy . . . and our first dinner was like a dinner of two close friends. It was really wild. He met me and thought he had met Mia."

But she was still reluctant about the role. "I was really shy about doing it. I was really nervous, and I was in a weird place in my life. And he convinced me, he made me feel fearless again."

And she is fearless on screen, brazen and vulnerable, the cocaine-snorting wife of a black millionaire mobster, looking like Anna Karina in *Vivre sa vie* (1962) or *Bande à part* (1964), Tarantino's favorite film of Godard, where Karina has a helmet of black hair (Tarantino and Lawrence Bender would name their production company A Band Apart, with a wink to Godard, and a colophon showing silhouettes of Michael Madsen, Steve Buscemi, Tim Roth, and Harvey Keitel, the four main Reservoir Dogs). Though Uma stars in only one of the three tales, her "date" with Vincent Vega is at the heart of *Pulp Fiction,* providing its funniest and scariest moments, as she dances the twist with him, overdoses on his bag of heroin, and comes to life again as a female Frankenstein.

Tarantino likes to speak of Uma Thurman as his "Marlene Dietrich," playing upon Austrian director Josef von Sternberg's hypnotic hold over Marlene, shaping and reshaping her in films such as *Morocco, Shanghai Express, The Scarlet Empress,* and *The Devil Is a Woman,* bathing her in an atmosphere of smoke and clouds, catching her at her very best angles, lighting her the way no actress had ever been lit before . . .

But the real difference is that Tarantino doesn't fetishize Uma Thurman; he allows her to look and play rather than to be looked at. She's much closer to Anna Karina than to Marlene. She's part of an ensemble, and she's isn't meant to overpower or dazzle us, or be lit up like some goddess. Cultural critic bell hooks calls her Marsellus's "lying, cheating lapdog white child-woman wife." And hooks doesn't have much more sympathy for Samuel L. Jackson (Jules) and his "Jheri Curls" (the sign of a black man who hates his own blackness). But if Mia and Marcellus and Jules are part of a retro culture that constantly recycles itself and all its junk, Tarantino himself is a master at processing this junk, so that Jack Rabbit Slim's, the 1950s retro diner where we meet Marilyn Monroe and Mamie Van Doren look-alikes and Mia has a Martin and Lewis milkshake, is a cavern that becomes the ultimate movie palace, where customers can sit among their very own icons and play with them.

An anonymous reviewer in the *Sunday Telegraph* goes even further than bell hooks in calling Tarantino "a dorky white boy" whose work is one enormous act of minstrelsy: "as much as the nineteenth-century Christy Minstrels rubbing burnt cork on their faces for the amusement of middle-class whites, movie violence is about appropriating real pain and transforming it into a vaudeville turn. Tarantino is the master, the greatest poseur in a poseur's culture."

Pulp Fiction is about vaudeville, about pure play, and we do watch Jules dispatch several yuppie drug dealers who tried to cheat Marcellus; we are "distanced" from their deaths, but it has less to do with vaudeville than with the fact that we are mesmerized by Jules; we can't take our eyes off him. He obliterates everyone else in the scene, including

John Travolta. *Pulp Fiction* succeeds in large part because of Samuel L. Jackson's performance as the philosophical hit man who quotes from Ezekiel before killing one of the yuppies. Does it really matter what sources Tarantino used, that he was referring to Sonny Chiba, the Japanese martial arts movie star, who would recite a sermon to his enemies before knocking them off in *Shadow Warriors,* his hit television series?

It's not Sonny Chiba we dream of as we watch Jules. He can misquote Ezekiel as much as he likes. He's still *our* "Son of a Preacher Man," to quote from one of the songs on the soundtrack. We adore John Travolta in the film, but our relation to Jackson is much more complex: we fear him and want him never to go away. Owen Gleiberman in *Entertainment Weekly* says that Jackson "reigns over *Pulp Fiction,*" with his "raw ferocity . . . He just about lights fires with his gremlin eyes, and he transforms his speeches into hypnotic bebop soliloquies." He is "fury reined in by order."

"I wrote the part of Jules for Samuel Jackson," Tarantino told Michel Ciment and Hubert Niogret of *Positif.* "I knew he gave off an incredible feeling of power and that, if given the possibility, he could express this Richard III side of himself that he has in the film. There are not a lot of actors who can dominate a scene, move people around the room like pawns in a chess game without even standing up, just sitting there [as

Jackson did in the final scene, with Pumpkin and Honey Bunny]. And that's what Sam does in *Pulp Fiction*."

It's the same scary perfection and interior life that Michael Madsen delivered as Mr. Blonde, but we're glad when Blondie is blown away, and we'd mourn Jules through eternity if he didn't survive *Pulp Fiction*. But Jackson is no fool. He grasped the unique force and rhythms of Tarantino's material. "I sat down, read the script straight through, which I normally don't do, took a breath, then read it again, which I never do, just to make sure it was true. That was the best script I'd ever read. . . . When people see killers for hire, they tend to think that they sit at home, they clean their guns, they sharpen their knives, they polish their bullets and all these other things. But Quentin takes you into a world where you actually find out that they gossip. They talk about their lives outside of what they do."

And we're willing to follow this Son of a Preacher Man, even if we fall with him into some horrendous hole . . .

CHAPTER FOUR
Negative Space

1.

*P*ulp Fiction would have a fate like that of no other film, except for *Citizen Kane*, which arrived like an irregular rocket in a country that would soon go to war. But there was no film culture when *Kane* was released, no American critics who could map the originality of what Welles had done, or describe *Kane*'s grammar—films weren't supposed to have a grammar or a language of their own. There was no understanding of "negative space," as film critic Manny Farber would define in 1971: "a sense of terrain created partly by the audience's imagination" and by the constantly shifting construct of "camera-actors-director," with the director "testing himself" as he moved across the void of his own landscape. "[A] movie filled with negative space is always a textural work throbbing with acuity." And Welles's lifelong quest was to mark this terrain, "make it prismatic and a quagmire at the same time." But Hollywood didn't believe in quagmires, and it didn't believe in *Kane*.

The film was lost for ten years and didn't surface again until the fifties, when a small gang of French critics that included André Bazin, co-founder of *Les Cahiers du Cinéma*, began to insist that there was such a thing as "film history," and that *Kane* was one of the masterworks of this new art form that so few people had ever bothered to talk about.

Bazin understood the monstrosity of *Kane*, the boldness of a film that was willing to break every Hollywood rule, to push into some unchartered territory where one could not "separate the actor from the decor, the foreground from the background," and where each individual moment recapitulated the entire film, where objects like a glass or spoon could take on their own magical personae, where the narrative moved in constant swirls rather than along a continuous line, where you had rip after rip in the "seamless web" of storytelling that moguls like Louis B. Mayer loved so much. *Kane* was about amnesia; we learn less and less as we plunge deeper into the film.

There was a gigantic hole in the screen that Welles wouldn't "suture" over with the connective tissue and lyricism of a completed life. "Rosebud" (Kane's last spoken word), the clue that drives the film, is nothing but a trick in a great big bag of tricks; and when "Rosebud" is revealed as the name of his childhood sled, a childhood that was wrenched from him, this revelation is one more shadow in a film of shadowlands. And if we aren't careful, we could fall into that hole in the screen, with Welles and Charles Foster Kane . . .

Even if Hollywood was the land of forgetfulness, of no risks, it would never be the same. It could thwart Welles, closet his film, turn him into an outlaw, a wanderer who had to beg for money to keep working, but it couldn't bury the fact that *Kane* was the first studio film (made at RKO) that defied the studio system. Welles was no hired gun delivering a piece of merchandise. And Tarantino could never have said that cinema was "an art form . . . not a textile plant," without the example of Welles and *Citizen Kane*.

Welles couldn't save himself, but the "myth" of *Kane* proved more powerful than the moguls themselves, most of whom disappeared by the end of the fifties (Jack Warner lingered a bit, swearing that he could tell the worth of a film by how much of it he could watch before he had to take a leak). Suddenly there were film schools and a new generation of filmmakers that cared more about Welles than the memory of Louis B. Mayer. This generation flourished in the seventies, while the studios floundered, frightened of its audiences, which had lived through Vietnam and wanted some image of themselves on the screen rather than Mary Poppins. And so we had *Taxi Driver, Chinatown, The Conversation, Five Easy Pieces,* and *Shampoo,* before Steven Spielberg, the most ingenious movie man of his generation, directed *Jaws* (1975) with all the brilliance and cunning of Barnum & Bailey.

It was like sitting in a circus, a circus without the least bit of "negative space" or ambiguous territory. And the American New Wave, which had schooled itself on Welles and Godard and Truffaut, couldn't compete with this circus. Hal Ashby and Peter Bogdanovich, together with Scorsese and Coppola, soon fell into the dark, with Scorsese the only real survivor. And Tarantino may talk about the influence of Dario Argento and Mario Bava and their horror films, he may even name a brand of heroin in *Pulp Fiction* after Bava, and swear allegiance to Sergio Leone and John Woo, but he was formed by the American New Wave and its belief in no surrender to the studios and their bankers, or to the stars, who were gathering more and more strength as "ex-slaves," no longer bound to a studio by seven-year contracts. Tarantino was merciless, as Welles had once been. Welles took on *all* the moguls by poking fun at one of their own, modeling Kane on William Randolph Hearst, a newspaper tycoon who was a king with his own castle, San Simeon (called Xanadu in *Kane*), where he presided over Hollywood's royalty with his mistress, movie star Marion Davies. Welles not only turned Marion into a no-talent opera singer, he took the tycoon's pet name for her private parts, "Rosebud," and used it as a kind of key to enter *Kane*, while the whole of Hollywood laughed at Welles's dirty little joke.

But that wasn't his greatest sin against the moguls; he defied their raison d'être, their hierarchy of beliefs, with his film. Welles insisted that audiences wake up from their slumber in the moviehouse and enter into the puzzle of Charles Foster Kane, that they respond to the gaps and "wounds" in the screen, and become part of the film's terrain. The moguls didn't want anything wild that would upset their little ordered lives; Hollywood's most brilliant producer, Irving Thalberg, had once "tamed" the Marx Brothers by cutting out their best gags and telling them that a film couldn't have too many laughs . . .

Kane is a sarabande of moments and set pieces—flashbacks within a flashback, a newsreel, a succession of breakfast scenes in which Kane and his first wife age in front of our eyes—that overpower the film, force us to contemplate its structure, and hold us in its thrall. We have no idea of what is coming next; *Kane* composes and decomposes in front of our eyes, builds and destroys and builds again; characters die and grow young in the next scene, until time itself becomes a liquid that can flow anywhere.

Tarantino's second film has much of the same liquid; Travolta is shot to pieces and then comes back to play with us. Tarantino says he doesn't like flashbacks, but he has Butch

the boxer (Bruce Willis) recall his father's gold watch in a
dream that's just like a flashback. But the camera remains
neutral, however bizarre the moment, and never heightens
the action, never tricks us into seeing what we don't want to
see. Horrors abound in the film—Vincent accidentally shoots
one of the yuppie dealers in the face, Marcellus is raped by a
redneck, Marcellus shoots the same redneck in the groin after
Butch rescues him by slicing the redneck's accomplice with a
samurai sword, Vincent has to stab Mia in the chest with a
needle of adrenaline that looks like a knife—but we never
seem to stray far from comedy. We don't grieve for Marvin
(the young black man Vincent has killed), because he's never
really been *inside* the frame. And critics who want to see this
as a kind of cultural tyranny where whites can "off" blacks
and butt-fuck them, in Tarantino's own version of "white
cool," are forgetting that whites fare no better in this particular dance.

The very best comedies are often cruel and filled with
outrageous burlesque, where all the characters are victims
and victimizers, where everything and everyone is a target,
and we end up in the same "Duck Soup," whether the
author is Aristophanes, the Marx Brothers, or Mel Brooks
(in *Young Frankenstein* and *Blazing Saddles*). And in Tarantino's Duck Soup, "realities tumble one into the other—race
into race, class into class—and make us realize, once more,

how little separates us in our urban Wild West of contra-band, drugs, bribery, and professional destruction," writes Stanley Crouch.

Such was the furor surrounding *Pulp Fiction* that *ArtForum* devoted a hefty portion of its March 1995 issue to puncturing the film's critical balloon in articles entitled "Geek Chic, "Cool Tool," "Minor Magic," and "Slick Shtick." This was no ordinary hatchet job; the articles are lively and intelligent, and their authors—Gary Indiana, bell hooks, Dennis Cooper, and Robin Wood—have impeccable credentials as purveyors of film culture and guardians of the *new,* and they all have at least a grudging respect for Tarantino's art and a willingness to interpret whatever language he has or doesn't have. "[Tarantino's] movies are formulaic but the formula is unique, a wild collision of things—the rupture of narrative time, rougher and more radical than Godard's . . . Tarantino can invest a cliché with breathless energy," writes Gary Indiana, who articulates Tarantino's greatest sin. "One is always inside an artifact cobbled from other artifacts rather than from any profound experience of life." And, says Dennis Cooper, "Tarantino really is one of the few post-Martin Scorsese directors capable of bona fide cinematic magic." But, "Scorsese is deep, and his best films are girded with emotional and spiritual scars," while "Tarantino gives terrific surface."

Bell hooks calls him "a master deconstructivist" with a "post-Modern flavor." And she would identify Tarantino's Duck Soup of races and realties bumping into each other as "multiculturalism with a chic neofascist twist." She zeroes in on Jules (Samuel L. Jackson) as a "death-dealing mummified intellectual" with a "retro hairdo" that's "like a minstrel thing—telling the world that the black preacher philosopher is ultimately just an intellectual arty white boy in drag, aping, imitating, and mouthing intellectual rhetoric that he can't quite use to help him make sense of his own life." And Jules' creator is one more "dead white-boy star-culture bandit."

Bell hooks is absolutely right . . . and wrong. Jules is a specter out of minstrelsy. And his hairdo is "his own signifying monkey . . . That hair is kinda like another character in the film. Talking back to Jules as he talks to us, it undermines his words every step of the way." That is, unless the parameters shift and we are living in a comic universe, a land of pure play, where shibboleths such as "deep" or "profound life experience" might have a little less magic than we would like to think.

Jules' philosophy does come out of the junk shop of pop culture. He wants to walk the earth, "like Caine in *Kung Fu.* Just walk from town to town, meet people, get in adventures." He realizes that he and Vincent ought to be dead. The yuppie drug dealers had a "Fourth Man" hiding in their bathroom with a "huge silver .357 Magnum." The Fourth Man burst out of the bathroom, fired point-blank at Jules and Vincent . . . and missed every shot.

"It could be God stopped the bullets, he changed Coke into Pepsi," Jules says to Vincent. "You don't judge shit like that based on merit. Whether or not what we experienced was an according-to-Hoyle miracle is insignificant. What is significant is I felt God's touch. God got involved."

And because he "felt God's touch," Jules decides not to kill Pumpkin and Honey Bunny, as Tarantino rides us right back to the robbery at the coffee shop, where the film began. And the two pairs of "robbers"–Jules and Vincent, Pumpkin and Honey Bunny–are like crazy reflections of one another. Both teams steal identities–wallets or lives–and when they collide, it's almost as if they soften and soothe one another's rage. Pumpkin and Honey Bunny can leave with all the wallets (and Jules's cash, but not his "Bad Motherfucker" wallet), and Jules and Vincent can leave in the dorky costumes they had to put on after their ritualistic black suits were splattered with Marvin's blood and brain tissue. They look like clowns, and they are clowns, and I prefer them to any "profound life experience."

Bell hooks is "correct-amundo," as Jules himself might say, when she tells us that "our resident enlightened dharma bum

[Jules] has nowhere to go—no third world playground he can retire to," that he can only retire into "nothingness," but that doesn't diminish the demonic power of Jackson's perform-ance (hooks herself calls it "stunning"). No other actor has ever thrilled us so much, or lived inside the skin of the person he's playing with such heat. And that heat is outside any cul-tural barometer, or strict interpretation. Perhaps cinema itself is an art of surfaces: the shimmering bits of light on screen and the crackles of sound may be all the clues we'll ever have to anyone's interior life.

2.

S urfaces seem to be on everybody's mind, at least when they talk about Tarantino: he's postmodernism's own original stepchild, as if there was a hollowness at the heart of his work, and Tarantino himself was some mischievous lep-rechaun who went around polishing the same old surfaces again and again. In a full-length study of *Pulp Fiction,* Dana Polan describes postmodernism's "culture of surfaces," and its "rendering of a viscerality so intense that it substitutes for all concern with deep meaning." He likens *Pulp Fiction* to Dis-neyland and says that watching the film can be compared to a visit at a theme park. "There is in both activities the sense that the trajectory one follows is made up of a series of individual attractions, each of which sets out to surprise and dazzle." And these individual attractions "set themselves off from the plot to become stand-alone bits of virtuosity either in the craft of the dialogue, the weirdness of the action—as in the redneck pawnshop—or in the show-off quality of the cinematic style."

And I wonder what theme park Polan would find for *Citizen Kane.*

Pulp Fiction is worlds away from a Disneyland that might surprise and dazzle, but does not subvert or wander into any kind of real ruin. Tarantino began to call himself the Weinsteins' Mickey Mouse after Miramax was sold to Michael Eisner. But the original Mouse was a much more subversive creature, sounding like a boy soprano close to hysteria (Walt Disney supplied his voice), and not the little saint who presides over Disneyland . . .

Polan tries to unravel the differences between modern and postmodern, and in doing so he undermines the visceral power of cinema, its *need* for surfaces. "The enigma of modernism points toward higher meaning; those of postmodernism stay at the surface and make of the spectator a game-player." But the "text," whether it be a film or a novel, has always been a kind of game, where the reader of the text, modern or not, had to be involved in its internal rules and rhymes. The text is never stable, never solid or safe. It keeps erupting and moving out from under us, like a volcano, or it dies within the idiom of its own day, lost in the local color of one language or another, like some maddening hiero-glyphics. We can read *Hamlet* or *Gulliver's Travels* or the *Alice* books, because their personae and their language swell and shrink with a strange elasticity, and are monsters of the imag-ination in the magic theater that grows between ourselves and the text, our very own "negative space."

Postmodern has become a catchword for anything that's irregular or "unreal." In "Postmodernism: Roots and Poli-tics," sociologist Todd Gitlin sees beyond this irregularity. The premodern, he tells us, "cherishes continuity, speaking with a single narrative voice or addressing a single visual center. It honors sequence and causality in time and space." The modern work of art still seeks unity, but this unity is "assembled from fragments, or shocks . . . It shifts abruptly among a multiplicity of voices, perspectives, materials." But there is still a longing for wholeness at the center of things. That center is lost in postmodern art. Not only has the master voice dissolved, but any sense of loss is rendered deadpan. We now have an endless landscape of surfaces, "reverber-ating onto other surfaces." The text seems to be talking to itself, and is totally self-absorbed. It is "fragmented, unstable, even decomposed." Passion and beauty have become pack-aged materials, bits of decoration.

"Postmodernists ransack history for shards because there is no here here;" we no longer have any historical context; we ourselves have become packaged, like culture itself. We're the walking wounded, the reader of signs that never stop replicating in a culture of hype and hucksterism. We have come to view ourselves as products, as being more dead than alive.

Film is an American art, whether it was invented in America or not. It arrived with a new century, and the first global village, Hollywood, was made up of ragpickers and glove cutters like Louis B. Mayer and Samuel Goldwyn (or Goldfish), who couldn't go into banking and went into the brand-new business of motion pictures. They fabulated a town in a lemon grove, where they would have enough sunshine to shoot outdoors and indoors, and began producing their shadow plays, where anonymous actors would parade like ghosts on a screen. These moguls longed for love stories to captivate their audiences, but the moviehouse was also a mausoleum; audiences could read their own deaths in the darkness that began and ended every film. But with all that movement, all that jumping around, they could forget that they were in the land of Osiris. They had Gary Cooper to die for them, or Jean Gabin (if they were French). They had Garbo to leave her own isolation and kiss John Gilbert before she went back into the gloom. They had Carole Lombard to make them laugh, even when they could feel a certain heart-break in her eyes. But it all seemed under control. The moguls had their love machines, gods and goddesses who lived like prisoners in the Hollywood hills.

And then came Orson Welles and his poisoned fairy tale, which mocked the moguls, mocked Marion Davies, mocked William Randolph Hearst, revealed his bedroom secrets, turned Marion's "Rosebud" into a child's sled, and made certain that audiences could share a little of Kane's death, as Welles pulled them deeper and deeper into the dark . . .

But if *Kane* was a time bomb for the moguls, a hint that an art form had grown up right under their noses, *Pulp Fiction* would explode upon a Hollywood that was still a self-enclosed world fifty years after *Kane* and no less ruthless and cowardly. Bell hooks reads Hollywood as "the place where white-supremacist capitalist patriarchy can keep inventing itself . . . Hollywood is the new plantation, getting more chic with the times." But she gives the film capital a little too much credit. And if we leap beyond her own ideology, we might read Hollywood as a corporate kingdom that's a bit like the Emerald City of Oz, where a bunch of frightened wizards hold on to their bag of tricks and try to feed the entire planet some ideal of a homogenized America.

For these wizards, *Kane* was un-American, *Kane* excoriated the American dream, exposed the narrowness of success, and concerned itself with camera angles and sound tricks that were beyond their comprehension. They killed the film as best they could; their own vassals would allow Welles to win only *one* Academy Award, for best original screenplay, which he had to share with Herman Mankiewicz, as if his own vision had been skewered from the start, and Welles was nothing but a half-man.

Tarantino would fare no better than Welles at the Academy Awards. He was "gumped" along with everybody else, as Robert Zemeckis' *Forrest Gump,* a film about an idiot savant who rolls across American history, won most of the major awards. Like Welles before him, Tarantino had to share his lone award (with Roger Avary, for best original screenplay). Hollywood preferred a heartbreaker like *Gump* rather than a film with raucous dialogue, dead bodies, and a hero who loves heroin. And there was, Tarantino realized, a good deal of resentment against Miramax and the Weinsteins, hooligans from Queens.

"At the end of the day, the studios don't like these intruders coming ːnto the business . . . like, if all the studio people had Thanksgiving—Miramax would have to sit at the kids' table." But the success of *Pulp Fiction* would soon change things. "Now, not only is Miramax sitting at the big table, but everyone's watching what they're eating."

Yet *Pulp Fiction* might have had no marketing strategy if not for France. *Reservoir Dogs* had been a kind of bastard at Cannes in 1992, when Tarantino was pampered like a puppy, while his film wasn't eligible to win any of the awards. Now it was 1994, and Tarantino's second film was part of the official competition, but Krzysztof Kieslowski's *Three Colors: Red* was favored to win. Kieslowski was ill, and had announced that *Red* would be his last film. He was a master at the end of his career, a master who could use sound and color like a great magician, and Tarantino was a rockabilly with renegade producers. But no one had counted on the Weinsteins in Cannes. They hit the beach like commandos, with *Pulp Fiction*'s entire cast. Cannes went crazy over John Travolta and Bruce Willis, but it was Tarantino himself who would become the star of this "*Pulp Fiction* posse"; not a soul had seen the film, which would have its premier at the festival, but the French had been the first to write about *Reservoir Dogs,* and "fans made a fuss over him wherever he went."

Miramax was on the move. It arranged lunches and dinners with "the *Pulp Fiction* posse" and certain critics. It arranged a private screening for them at the Olympia theater. And people at the screening, recalls Samuel L. Jackson, expected "some gorefest that was just bullets, guns and 'motherfucker, motherfucker,'" and here was something "that was totally new and unique . . . I had never seen the film until that first night. I had read it like 80, 90 times, but I was still overwhelmed sitting there, being in the presence of it."

"The *Pulp Fiction* posse" had packed its bags, certain that Kieslowski would win, when festival officials advised Harvey Weinstein to stay. It would be pandemonium. When Steven Soderbergh won the Palme d'Or for *sex, lies & videotape* in 1989, he noted that "it was as if a fairy had waved a wand and said, 'You're John Lennon for three hours.' "

Tarantino's three hours haven't ended yet. The Palme d'Or gave him "The Good Housekeeping Seal of Approval," he said. But it would give him more than that. It would authenticate him, allow him to perform, to become the Quentin Tarantino show, and he would take that show around the world. The first stop was Manhattan, but he needed a little help from John Travolta. The Weinsteins wanted to open *Pulp Fiction* as a vacation-time movie, as their summer hit, but Travolta fought against the plan. He had shouting matches and shoving wars with the Weinsteins. "You can't fuck around with this movie," he told Harvey Weinstein. "[Quentin] showed me more love than anyone has, ever, and I'm going to show him more love now by telling you you must protect him. You've won at Cannes, you saw those critics, I know those critics, this is bigger than you even know. You have to release this in October," with films that would compete for the Oscars.

No longer targeted as a summer hit, *Pulp Fiction* could open the New York Film Festival in September and create an immediate furor. Richard Peña, the festival's director, worried about all the violence. He could have picked a less controversial film for the coveted opening slot. "There was a certain amount of trepidation on all our parts." But Peña realized right away that *Pulp Fiction* "was just such a quantum leap over almost anything happening in American independent cinema."

When the film opened "wide" in October (on twelve hundred screens), it was already visible *after* the Palme d'Or and the promotion it received at the New York Film Festival. *The Specialist,* starring Sharon Stone and Sylvester Stallone, had opened the very same week, and should have been the monster hit of the season, but *Pulp Fiction* was number one at the box office, "and no one believed it," Tarantino told the *New York Times*. And then, after that first week, "we killed them." It was no act of divine intervention, as Jules might say. *Pulp Fiction* would prove to be the kiss of death for Stallone and his deadpan action-adventure films. Endless repetitions of Rocky-Rambo couldn't compete with Tarantino's miraculous revival of Abbott and Costello as Vincent and Jules. Stallone also plays a hit man (and demolition expert) whom Sharon Stone wants to hire. One almost wishes they could leave their laughable dialogue and grotesque turns of plot, run off to Jack Rabbit Slim's, and dance the twist . . .

Tarantino could defeat *The Specialist* and a hundred other

forgettable films, but he had a harder time grappling with himself. (Oliver Stone's *Natural Born Killers* had opened that summer, with Tarantino's original screenplay revised by Stone and two other writers.) He began to brood about Oliver Stone. "You can't just change my work and expect me to say it's okay." He was just being Quentin Tarantino. Tony Scott had monkeyed with *True Romance,* made it much more linear, but Scott wasn't a rival, and Oliver Stone was. Stone had started out as a screenwriter, like Tarantino himself; Stone had worked on *Scarface* (1983) with Brian De Palma, the first director Tarantino had ever really admired; Stone had gone to film school, and Tarantino was a video-store geek; Stone was the most admired filmmaker of the '80s and early '90s, with *Platoon, Wall Street, Born on the Fourth of July,* and *JFK.*

"To me the best thing about him is his energy. But his biggest problem is that his obviousness cancels out his energy and his energy pumps up his obviousness. He's Stanley Kramer with style"—meaning a director very much involved with his own message.

Whatever its "message," or its politics, *JFK* is a film about hallucination rather than history, filled with polymorphous voices: Jack Lemmon and Ed Asner are almost unrecognizable in their sordidness, and Gary Oldman plays Lee Harvey Oswald with a chill—a wildness—that's beyond the power of impersonation. These characters are ghosts packed into a universe where time has frozen around a murdered king, as much of America seemed ghostlike after Kennedy's assassination. It's hard to imagine that Tarantino didn't learn from *JFK,* or feel close to the gargoyles who haunt the screen. But he himself would haunt Oliver Stone, since *Pulp Fiction* opened worldwide before *Natural Born Killers,* and Stone kept appearing in Tarantino's tracks.

"In Europe and everywhere we went, we'd arrive in a country and [Quentin] had just been there [with *Pulp Fiction*], so at any interview we were getting these questions . . . What did you do to his sacred script? . . . So it hurt the business because it put a stain on the movie, as if the writer had walked out on it and that therefore it was a disaster. And he'd not even seen the movie. It was hardly fair. His hubris was enormous."

And Stone felt obliged to talk about *Pulp Fiction.* "The question is, can you expand his worldview beyond that genre, the combination of violence and humor? . . . You can't dine out on [pop-culture icons] for the rest of your life, in my opinion. You can make fun movies, or pulpy movies, but I don't know, is there really something being said?"

He was disturbed by the Tarantino mania that had hit half the planet. "I've never seen in my lifetime, this degree of reaction for a young filmmaker . . . I've never seen this. It's unbalanced. It's unnatural." And Tarantino had been particularly damaging to the reputation of *Natural Born Killers,* because he "became a god overnight, a myth, a legend. His is probably the most acclaimed single debut that I know of."

Except for Welles, who came riding out to Hollywood with his own theater company, the Mercury Players, and had a stint on the radio as "The Shadow," who could harm his enemies by hurling his voice; and there was also Welles's "War of the Worlds" broadcast, where he told of Martians landing in New Jersey the night before Halloween, and frightened the hell out of America. He was on the cover of *Time,* a twenty-three-year-old giant. He would prepare *Kane* at RKO while he romanced actress Dolores Del Rio, one of Hollywood's great beauties. He was brash, often a bully, a boy wonder who walked in a whirlwind of his own publicity. He was fond of magic tricks, and for a little while he seemed to make producers and moguls disappear at will. But he didn't understand the language of Hollywood. He thought he would have his toy trains at RKO forever. Being flamboyant, always prepared to shout and seduce, he had no instinct for studio politics or his own survival. And soon, very soon, Hollywood would bury him alive . . .

But Tarantino wasn't about to be buried: he's much more of an acrobat and a magician than Welles ever was. He would create his own production company with Lawrence Bender (and break up with Bender in 2005). He was always breaking up with everybody—agents, managers, girlfriends who had once helped his career. He understands the *business* of films in a way that Welles never could. He danced when he had to dance, courted interviewers until these same interviewers had to court him, traveled everywhere with his films until his films could travel on their own. Welles ended up a pauper scratching for money to make another film, and I doubt that Tarantino will ever have to scratch. "After *Pulp Fiction,* I never really have to work again if I don't want to, which is kind of a cool position," he told J. Hoberman.

Pulp Fiction made over two hundred million dollars worldwide. And as an ex-clerk, he could sense the importance of video sales. He delayed the video release of *Pulp Fiction,* knowing how hungry video stores and their customers would be for the film. And, said Tarantino, "it paid off big time!" When *Pulp Fiction* was finally released to the stores, "it ended up the best-selling priced-for-rental video in history, leapfrogging *Terminator 2, Dances with Wolves,* and *Ghost,* I think."

Yet his play at being a mogul is one more mask. He's as uncompromising a filmmaker as Welles, or Stanley Kubrick, who worried over every marketing detail of his films. And strategy alone couldn't have launched *Pulp Fiction* as the first independent film to perform like a Hollywood blockbuster.

Tarantino was indeed Miramax's Mickey Mouse . . . and a

lot, lot more. Harvey Scissorhands was the perfect counterpart to Tarantino—both of them are "800-pound gorillas," gorillas who know how to play with one another. "I am so happy I convinced you to use Travolta in this film," Harvey said, once he saw a rough cut of *Pulp Fiction*. But neither of them could have predicted that it would become a badge and a war cry for an entire generation of filmgoers, and a document that would mark the millennium.

Pulp Fiction has puzzled and perturbed filmmakers other than Oliver Stone. Paul Schrader sees a "big difference" between Tarantino and himself. "I mean, I'm really of the existential tradition, the twentieth-century tradition. Tarantino is tying into the ironic hero . . . Everything in the ironic world has quotation marks around it. You don't actually kill somebody; you 'kill' them. It doesn't really matter if you put a baby in front of the runaway car because it's only a 'baby' and it's only a 'car.' "

And thus we come back to Marvin, the young black dealer who is "accidentally" shot in the face and seems to disappear from our psyche. Ella Taylor calls Tarantino a master of manipulation, and he is manipulating us here. But he also shows our need to "suture," to cover over any horror with narrative. If we stayed with Marvin, we too would be stuck. We move on, concerned about what Jules and Vincent will do with a corpse in their car. It's almost as if amnesia is built into any narrative line; and perhaps we are all little caliphs, waiting for Scheherazade to continue her tale, while we forget what her last tale was about . . .

But it isn't only that. A major portion of "modern" narrative art, from *Don Quixote* to *Dead Souls,* from *The Castle* to *Waiting for Godot,* from *Breathless* to Lars Van Trier's *Dogville,* is about a numbing of emotion, a displacement into dream and artifact, as if the bare white lines of the town that Van Trier builds for us serve as a prison, or a carapace, that locks out all feeling, abandons us to an hallucinated world. And perhaps the leap into the postmodern is the building of such a carapace, where artifact replaces the rendering of ordinary life.

In Thomas Pynchon's *V.,* one of the first postmodern novels, Benny Profane, a total schlemiel, feels stranded "in the aisles of a bright, gigantic supermarket, his only function to want." Statues can talk in Pynchon's landscape, while humans are frozen inside a language they cannot decipher. Yet *V.* is all about language, about a structure that captures and imprisons, while Pynchon's characters permutate, crawl through time and space. It's a deeply pessimistic book. History has become nightmare, irrational and irreal; all that is left is play. Language, Roland Barthes tells us in *Writing Degree Zero,* has moved outside history, into the realm of dream and menace. And it's this menace, this deadly play, that preoccupies the postmodern, where the only belief is in the text. "Strings of language extend in every direction to bind the world into a rushing ribald whole," writes Donald Barthelme in "The Indian Uprising," where wars and realities mix and all ideologies are without meaning. "Some people," says a certain Miss R., "run to conceits of wisdom but I hold to the hard, brown, nutlike word."

Tarantino is like a brilliant anteater who's sucked in all the debris around him and hurls it back at us, as Donald Barthelme did in story after story. Jules's religious conversion, his own ideology, is just a kind of language game fed on the junk of television and on local lore. What will he find when he walks the earth like Caine in *Kung Fu*? He will evaporate, with his beliefs. Even if *Pulp Fiction* does "take place in a parallel universe," as Dana Polan suggests, it's a universe that's all too parallel, all too familiar, filled with fast food, and hit men who have to "get into character," play out their roles, just as the narrator of "The Indian Uprising" is buffeted about by a maelstrom of words *and* performances: "Once I caught Kenneth's coat going down the stairs by itself but the coat was a trap and inside a Comanche who made a thrust with his short, ugly knife at my leg which buckled and tossed me over the balustrade through a window and into another situation."

Tarantino's characters are always moving "into another situation," and one of the great pleasures of *Pulp Fiction* is tying ourselves to a character's tail and going along for the ride. But it's not the ride of most other films, where we settle into some kind of narrative suspense, as if the screen was a simulacrum of our own lives. Tarantino won't permit us to forget that John Travolta is *playing* Vincent Vega, and that Vince may have his own particulars—his gold earring, his paunch, his long hair, his heroin habit, his quiet truculence—but he is also the sum of every other part Travolta has played. Travolta's entire career becomes "backstory," the myth of a movie star who has fallen out of favor, but still resides in our memory as the king of disco. We keep waiting for him to shed his paunch, put on a white polyester suit, and enter the 2001 Odyssey club in Bay Ridge, Brooklyn, where he will dance for us and never, never stop. Daniel Day-Lewis couldn't have woken such a powerful longing in us. He isn't part of America's own mad cosmology. He's a marvelous Hawkeye in Michael Mann's *Last of the Mohicans* (1992), but Hawkeye can never replace Tony Manero—an angel sitting on Vince's shoulder.

Vincent slinks around like a clumsy bear, but when he dances the twist at Jack Rabbit Slim's, we surrender ourselves to movie time, give up the notion and narrative thread of a hit man squiring his boss's wife; their actual dance may be closer to the choreography of Anna Karina's shuffle with her two bumbling gangster boyfriends in *Bande à part,* but even *that* reference is lost to us, and we're with Tony again; we laugh at Travolta, at his obvious decay, but more important, Travolta is laughing at himself, at the silliness of movie culture, which selects its iconic moments and shoves them out of all proportion, yet these same moments still define us. Tarantino's films are about the tyranny of this culture, the hold it has on us. Like his audience, he's a hothouse of references, forever on fire. And he's forged his films out of this fire.

Jack Rabbit Slim's was at the center of his very own firestorm. It's much more than a retro diner with waitresses who are replicas of Marilyn Monroe. Vincent eats a Douglas Sirk steak, "bloody as hell." Sirk was the quintessential director of the 1950s. *Magnificent Obsession* (1954) and *Written on the Wind* (1956) are irresistible love stories that marked the decade: they're full of sound and fury . . . and a whole lot of kitsch. And Jack Rabbit Slim's is a shrine to Sirk, to comic books, rock 'n' roll, and 1950s cars. As Vincent himself says of Slim's: "It's like a wax museum with a pulse rate."

"We spent a good part of the film's budget on this scene," Tarantino told the editors of *Positif.* It was a necessary extravagance, including the gigantic speedometer that serves as a dance floor. Tarantino wasn't trying to score points with his paraphernalia. Slim's is a cave—a busy, boisterous cave—that one can always find in Tarantino's films: the warehouse in *Reservoir Dogs;* the indoor shopping mall in *Jackie Brown;* and the House of Blue Leaves in *Kill Bill Vol. 1.* Slim's and the

House of Blue Leaves are like Rick's Café in *Casablanca,* a contraption of tinsel and papier-mâché that's as fraudulent as Hollywood itself, but where everybody goes.

"Quentin is not Jimmy Stewart," says Jennifer Beals. "The shadow side is definitely there, and he lets it out only when he needs it, like some kind of beast that gets fed only now and again, and then gets put back. That's what makes his films great. That's where his genius is."

And it's this "shadow side," this dark edge, that much of postmodernism is really about, whether we look for it in Roy Lichtenstein, Donald Barthelme, or Tarantino—it's a retreat into some wonderland that mirrors our culture with its own crazy glance. It's a flight from history and all its crusades, from the wholesale slaughter of the twentieth century, with its propaganda, its slogans, its hard, hard sell. If it flattens out the "real," and replaces it with pop icons, it's because these icons comfort us in a way that history never can. Lichtenstein's tearful maidens appropriated from the panels of True Romance comic strips, Barthelme's mock-heroic military men in "The Indian Uprising," and Jack Rabbit Slim's—all three share a sense of parody and ferocious play, a parody of our own pretensions, our seriousness, our sanctimony, our willingness to butcher in the name of belief . . .

Jack Rabbit Slim's is Tarantino's pleasure dome, where he has "the whole treasure of the movies to choose from and can take whatever gems [he likes], twist them around, give them new form, bring things together that have never been matched up before."

Movies, Tarantino is telling us, are all about appropriation, about stealing shadows from a wall. He learned to direct by watching other actors, by stealing from "Marlon Brando or Michael Caine." And doesn't Orson Welles appropriate the character of Kane from William Randolph Hearst, doesn't he steal Hearst's own sexual secrets, mock history by manufacturing a newsreel of Kane's rise and fall, doesn't he mock the moguls themselves by deconstructing Kane, robbing him of a reasonable life, and robbing Hollywood of the linear narrative it loves so much?

Kane is no less problematic than *Pulp Fiction,* no less of a minefield and a conundrum; both films take us deep into the night, into a landscape that slides out right from under us; both are filled with caverns: Kane's Xanadu is a mansion of mirrors where each persona, each image, breaks down into endless repetitions of itself, just as we break down as we watch ourselves in the endless mirrors of a moviehouse. Whatever their differences, Welles and Tarantino are "movie men" who have whisked us out of Hollywood's usual safety zones and into a very private place where they alone have been willing to go.

CHAPTER five
Shoot Me Like I'm Sharon Stone

1.

Tarantino would have his own wanderlust for the next three years. First he went around the world with *Pulp Fiction,* giving over six hundred interviews. "We showed *Pulp Fiction* in China. The government sanctioned it, and I've never seen a more enthusiastic response. When I went to introduce the movie, it was more like a rock concert than a movie. It was like freedom, a night of freedom." And Tarantino was a star *before* a single frame of *Pulp Fiction* was shown to his audience of film students: "the video piracy in Asia is just remarkable, so all the young kids had seen, or owned, video copies of the movie. The film students at the Beijing Academy totally knew who I was."

But after his six hundred interviews, Tarantino decided to take a leave of absence from film, a sabbatical year. "Life's just too short to do movie after movie after movie. It's like getting married just to get married." He didn't want to go the way of Rainer Werner Fassbinder (1946–1982), the most radical director of the New German Cinema. "I remember when I was younger I wanted to be like Fassbinder, forty-two films in ten years." But Fassbinder, who was eaten up by his own work, longed to rip apart *all* film language, even his own . . . with the help of cocaine. He would let his characters talk in front of a stationary camera until they hypnotized you, or drove you insane. He died of an overdose at thirty-six, disappearing into the bleak and barren landscape of his own images.

But Tarantino's sabbatical became "the busiest hiatus in the history [of Hollywood]." He was everywhere at once—on talk shows, behind the camera, in front of the camera (appearing in a sitcom that parodied *Pulp Fiction* or acting in the films of his friends). He was Johnny Destiny in Jack Baran's *Destiny Turns on the Radio,* and a drug mule in Robert Rodriguez's *Desperado* (both 1995). He was essentially playing himself, and welcomed his own foolishness, as if he'd become one more character in his menagerie, a character he could deconstruct. "[H]e relishes the challenge of being a pop figure in the middle of a pop cycle," according to Alexandre Rockwell.

The most brazen of his self-parodies was as Chester Rush, a megalomaniacal director in *Four Rooms* (also 1995), a compilation film he did with three other directors: Rockwell, Rodriquez, and Allison Anders, who was at Sundance with him. The idea had been brewing ever since *Reservoir Dogs:* four young directors who could hang out together and take their little film on the festival circuit. But something intervened: Tarantino's fame. It was "like making a film with Elvis Presley," Rockwell remembers. "When you work with Quentin, you can't try to rein him in. It'd be like trying to talk a crack addict out of robbing you. Basically, you just listen to him talk for two hours."

But two hours of talking couldn't salvage *Four Rooms,* which was supposed to take place on New Year's Eve at West Hollywood's own actors' hotel, the Chateau Marmont, called the Mon Signor in the film (Christopher Walken lives here when he's in Hollywood, and John Belushi died in one of its bungalows). There are four stories, in four different rooms, with a bellboy, modeled after Jerry Lewis, who weaves from room to room and presides over whatever narrative there is. Tarantino wanted Steve Buscemi to play the bellboy, but Buscemi declined; he must have sensed the idiocy behind the project. Tarantino then lured Tim Roth into the role. And Roth, who's never bad, who has a kind of resilient naturalness that he brings to every performance, tempting us, seducing us to *believe* in him, is terrible as Ted the bellhop. He has nothing to rub against except the silly fabric of four senseless tales.

He's forced to improvise, to shuffle, to laugh when there's

nothing to laugh about, as his accent shifts from Londoner to Los Angelino; he's a scarecrow in a bellhop's uniform, an animated ghost, but he can't liven up the proceedings. Rockwell and Tarantino have called him *Four Room*'s "fifth auteur," but fifth corpse would be a more accurate description. He cavorts in the penthouse with Chester Rush, who babbles about Jerry Lewis's miserly appreciation in America, and we feel as if we're entering a black hole: we can no longer listen. The film grows narrower and narrower and negates itself. Yet we linger with Chester Rush.

Larissa MacFarquhar says that Tarantino "loves actors' baggage of all sorts," their "backstory," the particular bump of their lives, and he realized that Chester Rush "ended up shouldering some of my own baggage as–for want of a better word–a celebrity." But *his* baggage is much more provocative than that. Even as we stop listening to Chester, we can feel Tarantino's need to be heard, like a child who's frightened of the dark and sings to us in order to soothe himself . . .

But it was another project with Robert Rodriguez–not the dreadful *From Dusk Till Dawn*–that was probably the most interesting aspect of his long "sabbatical." He began showing up in Austin, Texas, where Rodriguez lives and where film director Richard Linklater ran the Austin Film Society. He'd come to Austin in 1994 to present *Pulp Fiction* and fell in love with the town; he would hang out with Linklater and Rodriguez, drink Shiner Bock beer, gobble pizzas and chili, swim in the local pond, stay up all night, and find some "cave" where he could crash when he wasn't watching films.

He began collecting films the minute he had some money—obscure biker and horror films that no one had ever seen. He had these incredible prints, but no audience to build around them. "These prints are like my children, my babies, and it's not good enough just to show them to three or four people at my house." He approached Linklater about finding a venue where he could show his private collection, and that's how the Quentin Tarantino Filmfest was born. He descended upon the town in August 1996. What was meant to be a cozy weekend with Tarantino "turned into a week, then we tacked on the weekend after that week. It just got bigger and bigger."

He was under the same spell as his audience; the theater was packed with college kids (Austin is the state capital *and* seat of the University of Texas). "What tickles me is that people show up not even knowing what the movies are. They don't know what they're going to see, but they're excited about it. We haven't had a bad house."

He would have an "all-night horror marathon" and then have to repeat it because it was so popular. Tarantino himself was like a big goofy college kid among other college kids, and that's one of the reasons why younger audiences love him so much, whether he's in Austin or Beijing. He's half-formed, incomplete, with all the fears and expectations and obsessive wishes of a child, and such "wounds" inform his first two films, with their incessant chatter and the childlike stasis of characters who talk about sex but have so little appetite. Fear defines them: they're stuck in some kingdom where genitalia belong to other people, not themselves. And sex in Tarantino's films is parodied and played with, like a lost language.

"Butch?" Fabienne asks in *Pulp Fiction*. "Will you give me oral pleasure?"

And Butch answers, "Will you kiss it?"

She nods her head: *Yes*. "But you first."

It's the nearest we ever get to a sex scene. Any other film-maker would have had Vincent's "date" with the boss's wife end in bed. But Tarantino resists romance, even though romance is built right into Vincent's marathon dance with Mia at Jack Rabbit Slim's. It's the void around which he carves his characters, defying our expectations. And if there's something virginal about Tarantino, as Larissa MacFarquhar suggests, there is also something arrogant and brutal (like any child without brothers and sisters) particularly after *Pulp Fiction* plummeted Tarantino into a world where everybody wanted him. "Opening night [at the Austin Filmfest] was a little hysterical, but it was like 'OK, I'm in your town, now get over it.'"

And he no longer wanted to be photographed like a film geek or a champion of crime films, pointing a gun at his own head (as he appears in one of the Filmfest photos). "No, no, no, I'm not gonna lay in a bucket of blood and I'm not going to put my face against a brick and you're not going to shoot me with a razor blade in my mouth or pins in my face. You're going to shoot me like I'm Sharon Stone."

He was becoming unbearable. "He already sees himself as Alfred Hitchcock or Orson Welles," said Alexandre Rockwell. And in 1997 he told the *New York Times*: "I became an adjective sooner than I thought I was going to . . . Every third script out there is described as 'Tarantino-esque.'"

But even while he pontificated he was working on a new film. The sabbatical that never really was a sabbatical had now completed itself. "I'm in a writing mode," he said to the students at the Filmfest. He would spend most of 1996 and part of '97 scribbling away at a script, turning Elmore Leonard's novel, *Rum Punch,* into *Jackie Brown,* moving the narrative and various lowlifes from Miami to Los Angeles' South Bay, where he could provide his own coloring, his own special funk. "I did not want it to look like a *Reader's Digest* version of [Leonard's] novel." Jackie Burke, a white airline hostess who had a hard edge and wasn't totally reliable, would become Jackie Brown, a black hostess who worked for "the shittiest little shuttle-fucking piece of shit Mexican airline that there is," had much bigger hips than Leonard's heroine and not so hard an edge . . .

2.

We catch a woman in profile, moving along a conveyor belt, with what seems to be a tile wall in the background, a wall of many colors, pale blue, aquamarine . . . The woman is wearing a blue uniform. She could almost be a cutout, a cardboard figure, a doll in a doll's tile world, except for the slight smile on her face. It's Pam Grier, the former queen of blaxploitation flicks, but she isn't fetishized, isn't blown up to reveal her beauty. While the belt moves along, we can hear the theme song to *Across 110th Street* (1972), a gangster movie that ranges through Harlem and pits a white and black cop (Anthony Quinn and Yaphet Kotto) against the Mafia, a black mob, and each other. It arrived during the "blaxploitation" wave, which had drawn a young black audience (mostly male) *out* of the ghettoes and into the moviehouses of major American cities. In *Baadasssss Cinema* (2002), a documentary that explores blaxploitation, Tarantino talks about his own discovery of the phenomenon. It was in the early seventies, and he was a little kid who ventured into a downtown LA "that was like a black Hollywood." Baadasssss films were showing in every single theater. "I felt like I was in a black world." He walked into a theater and what excited him was that there was no distance between the audience and the characters on screen. People cursed and cheered and poked fun of heroes and villains alike, talked back to the screen, possessed it, made it their home . . .

Across 110th Street tried to mirror blaxploitation, break into its audience, but it didn't have Richard Roundtree as Shaft, a baadasssss private detective, and it didn't have Pam Grier, who would play in *Coffy* (1973), *Foxy Brown* (1974), and *Sheba Baby* (1975), with a razor in her Afro and a gun in her bra. She was constantly gawked at by every character: her favorite costume was her own voluptuous body, with which she would lure some bad guy into bed and then snuff him out, avenging one of her own lost lovers. These films coupled violence with softcore pornography; the acting was atrocious; the camera was asleep except for glimpses at her body; the dialogue was imbecilic, but *Foxy Brown* was still great fun. Baadasssss Cinema had more energy and wit, more playfulness, more pluck, than Hollywood's big-star productions. *Foxy Brown* and *Black Caesar* (1973) would rivet Tarantino in the same way that "B" films of the forties had riveted Godard and given him the courage to shoot his films on the fly. And Tarantino's use of *Across 110th Street* serves as a kind of "backstory" to Pam Grier. It evokes Harlem, evokes Foxy Brown, but demystifies Baadasssss Cinema at the same time.

We're introduced to Jackie Brown as an icon on a treadmill; the more she moves, the more she seems to be standing still. Tarantino's fans were waiting for him to do another *Pulp Fiction,* but he didn't want to revisit Jack Rabbit Slim's. He seems to be offering us a meditation on the very idea of slowness, without *Pulp Fiction*'s sleight of hand. We're forced to examine Jackie and film itself without camera angles, without depth of field. And we realize that Tarantino is a constructionist who dreams in the abstract and fits his characters into whatever he happens to construct . . .

But we leave that tile wall and its monotonous motion: Jackie starts to run. We can recognize an airport. It's LA International. We still catch her in profile, but she's no longer a cutout, or an icon smiling at itself. We can almost feel her flesh. Jackie's a little late. She gets to the counter of her "piece of shit Mexican airline," smiles at a customer we never see, and says "Welcome aboard!"

Jackie could be talking to us. She's welcoming us aboard the film's own journey. And we're a little dazed: in five minutes of slow and quick motion, Tarantino has taken us across

Baadasssss Cinema, presented Jackie Brown, and prepared us for some rabbit hole—the adventure of falling into the dark of a film. But we never fall.

Jackie is absent from the next scene, and we mourn her absence. We're in Hermosa Beach with Ordell Robbie (Samuel L. Jackson) and Louis Gara (Robert De Niro), who's just got out of the clink and is wearing his jailhouse tattoos. He seems moribund, like a sleepy caveman, and we have to force ourselves to remember that this same actor was once lithe and lean, with a demonic beauty and grace—as young Vito Corleone, or Johnny Boy, who dances along the roofs in *Mean Streets,* and Travis Bickle, a psychopath who looks like a Renaissance prince in *Taxi Driver.* But here he's morose as he listens to Ordell natter about guns.

Ordell has "a long, plaited goatee beard, so thin it's barely visible at times." He's as much of an assassin as Jules Winn- field ever was, but we keep wishing he'd put on Jules's Jheri Curls and play with us. We're stuck with him and Louis, and a camera that seems to have no point of view, a camera that doesn't protect them the way it protected Pumpkin and Honey Bunny. Ordell and Louis are all alone.

Then the camera moves behind Ordell to reveal someone's legs: they belong to Melanie, Ordell's "little surfer girl," played by Bridget Fonda with a delightful snootiness. At least Melanie is alive: she's trying to seduce Louis right in front of Ordell. She puts her toes (covered with rings) next to his drink. She keeps ogling him. But Louis is "out to lunch," in his own dreamworld.

The camera finally offers us a point of view: we watch Louis and Ordell from Melanie's perspective—that is, the point of view of her legs. Melanie's toes are like little live animals, crawling toward Louis, enticing him.

"Boring, isn't it?" she says to Louis while Ordell is on the phone. "He ain't more of a gun expert than I am."

And we believe her, but not even Melanie's toes can rescue the scene and the neutrality of its domain. Tarantino wants us to "hang out" with his characters. The film "is about getting to know them, and the way you get to know them is by hanging out with them." It's "the old *Rio Bravo* thing," where Howard Hawks spoofs the whole idea of a storyline, whisks John Wayne and Dean Martin outside the narrative, lets them have some fun while *pretending* to be in a Western. So much of Tarantino's aesthetic comes from this film and from the notion that an actor's ultimate rehearsal is with the audience. Actors and actresses audition for us right on the screen, just as John Travolta "auditions" while he's dancing the twist. But we love John Travolta and John Wayne, and we want to hang out with them.

Tarantino calls *Jackie Brown* a "hangout movie," one we will relish for the rest of our lives. "Every two or three years, put in *Jackie Brown* again, and you're drinking white wine with Jackie, and drinking screwdrivers with Ordell, and taking bong hits with Melanie and Louis."

I doubt it. We might follow Jackie forever on her conveyor belt, but we'd like to get rid of Ordell and Louis as fast as we can. Tarantino is trapped in his own "text," and the neutral camera that surrounds Ordell and Louis in Hermosa Beach isn't the same sort of *slowness* that surrounds Jackie, protects her, nourishes her. Adapting Elmore Leonard didn't liberate Tarantino, it shoved him into the confines of a story about a sting operation, it saddled him with someone else's language and with characters he might embroider but who would never be part of his own menagerie, except for Jackie herself, because Pam Grier doesn't belong in anyone's novel: Pam Grier is . . . Pam Grier, with all the "baggage" that Tarantino loves so much. But the narrative that unfolds has few surprises. It's as if Tarantino were picking apart his own repertoire, reshuffling his bag of tricks. When Louis shoots Melanie in a parking lot for nagging him too much, it has none of the shock value of Jules shooting one yuppie dealer while he's talking to another. Still, that's only a minor sin. What "hurts" the film for me is the detailed mapping out of Jackie's plan to rid Ordell of half a million dollars and hoodwink an Alcohol, Tobacco and Firearms officer (Michael Keaton) at the same time. Jackie switches shopping bags in the dressing room of a designer clothing store at the Del Amo mall, and with the help of a bail bondsman, Max Cherry (Robert Forster), she makes off with most of the money.

Tarantino is a master at carving around a climactic event—the robbery in *Reservoir Dogs,* or Butch's boxing match in *Pulp Fiction*—but here we observe the switch of shopping bags from four points of view; Tarantino could be writing his own *Rashomon* as he reveals the unreliability of any one perspective. But there's *nothing* to reveal in the switch, *nothing* to learn from how it was choreographed. We've entered some land of dead space, where the cinematic machine is mocking its own movements in a ballet without an end, while we jump ahead of the narrative and leave all the characters behind. . . .

3.

Just when we're about to abandon the film, Jackie Brown returns on her conveyor belt. She's so powerful a presence, and Tarantino's camera is so unambiguous about her, that she rescues the film whenever it reaches into the doldrums or his camera goes astray, wandering into a world apart from Jackie Brown. She's much larger than the tale she is in. Jackie herself *is* the narrative, and so much of

Tarantino's magic comes from his devotion to her on screen, his ability to free her in front of an audience so that she can present herself rather than some performing mask. Tarantino wanted the memory of Foxy Brown, but he didn't want a black bombshell with a gun in her bra, an Amazon who could arrive and depart in various stages of undress.

Like a certain actress named Pam Grier, who had reached the point of invisibility during the past twenty years, had not starred in a single film since her Baadasssss days, Jackie Brown "has worked her way down the ladder [. . .] she has got nowhere to go." And Tarantino *plays* against her beauty. He has her "come on with no makeup, hair out to here," and forces her to find her own "safe place," where she can "really live and be Jackie." That is the wonder of the film, and not all the fake fury surrounding the abracadabra of disappearing dollars.

Because of the novel, Tarantino was suckered into stringing along a plot we couldn't care less about; he should have given up Elmore Leonard, kept Jackie on her conveyor belt, and continued his meditation on the art of slowness, with Fassbinder as his father. But it might have been too much, a film where every image grapples with the camera's own love of movement. Instead, he offers us a rather conventional caper that intrudes upon an unconventional love story where the lovers never touch, never kiss, until the last moments of the film.

Robert Forster as the bail bondsman is as wondrous as Pam Grier. He's another wrecked actor whom Tarantino brought back from oblivion. Critic Michael Fleming calls this part of Tarantino's Rediscovery Network, "giving second [and third] chances to actors long forgotten by everyone but him."

Forgotten actors inspired Tarantino's most trenchant remark when he told Larissa MacFarquhar: "Robert Forster's face is backstory." And it is. We can feel the whole history of him in his sad, sad eyes as he watches Jackie Brown swerve away from killers and cops. Jackie Burke is a much colder customer in the novel. And when Max Cherry doesn't run off with her, we know it's out of self-preservation. She would fleece him in the end, steal every pocket in his pants. But Jackie Brown's offer to Max is much more enticing. She isn't cold. She likes his companionship, wants him to leave his own shitty business and share her loot, but he can't. Her enthusiasm would only break him. Perhaps he can rise up from the dead, but not long enough to have a real sexual life with Jackie Brown . . .

Born and raised in Rochester, Robert Forster was a college athlete who stumbled into acting. His most *visible* perform-ance was as a mournful-looking TV cameraman in Haskell Wexler's *Medium Cool* (1969), a film that documents the confrontation between protestors and police at the 1968 Democratic Convention in Chicago; Forster seems in a trance during the bloodshed, but his own "medium cool" makes the events around him much more chilling, much more brutal. He soon vanished into television, appeared in several series, including *Banyon* (1972), where he was a stone-faced private detective in Raymond Chandler's Los Angeles (Banyon was like Philip Marlowe's own little lost brother). The show didn't last more than one season, yet Banyon was still one of Tarantino's boyhood heroes: he must have grown up with that haunted face in his mind. But haunted faces aren't part of America's fabric, and Forster slid from minor movie to minor movie.

"The last five years, I hadn't gotten a job for more than scale, and terrible, junky stuff that you take when you've got a kid in college and an ex-wife," Forster told Michael Fleming. "Then Quentin comes along and says, 'You've waited long enough. Now you're going to work again.' I can't describe the feeling."

But not everyone could be resurrected. "A lot of these actors, after they lose their heat, move to television or exploitation films. Sometimes that takes it out of an actor. But sometimes it doesn't, and they're hungry for new material. When they get it, you see that light in their eyes," said Tarantino.

He was considering several actors for the role of Max Cherry: Paul Newman, Gene Hackman, John Saxon . . . and

Forster. Then one day he walked into a restaurant to do a little work on *Jackie Brown* and Robert Forster happened to be sitting next to him. "That's Max Cherry, he's right there." And once Tarantino began to divine like some powerful magus, there was a certain inevitability about his choice: no one else could ever be Max. Forster and Pam Grier had regained their "heat," but in some subtle fashion that only the magus himself could predict. Disheveled, her hair awry, poignantly unglamorous in a prison suit, Pam Grier rides right above the myth of Baadasssss Cinema; and Max Cherry as her "lover" is able to occupy that void, that howling darkness all *serious* films have to enter if they want to capture us. Max and Jackie are Tarantino's most complicated couple. He doesn't cover them in comedy, or have them charm us with a riff; Jackie and Max live in their own silences, the space between sentences they cannot speak; they're always apart when they're together and with each other when they split. That's the paradox of *Jackie Brown,* a film about the intimacy of separation, about the strange ways of being together in Tarantino's cosmos. It's called "movie love," where a glance can be more vivid than as kiss, where an audience can bring along its own crayons and color in whatever complexity or entanglement it wants, as if we were all brilliant cartoonists filling in contours that are already there . . .

CHAPTER SIX

Don't Kill Bill

1.

Jackie Brown earned back its money—twelve million dollars—during its "maiden" week (it opened at the very end of 1997). America didn't fall in love with the film. It soon dropped out of sight, totaling just under forty million after week thirteen. But it still allowed Tarantino to declare his independence from the moguls. Like Kubrick, he was an original—a provocative director who watched where every single penny went. He wanted to make a twelve-million-dollar film that *looked* like twenty million. "You can't lose. You absolutely, positively can't lose. And you don't have to compromise."

This time there were no sabbaticals. Tarantino started to scratch away at the script of a World War II epic, *Inglorious Bastards,* meant for John Travolta. But he couldn't stop thinking about *his* actress: ever since *Pulp Fiction,* he wanted to work with Uma Thurman again. At Jack Rabbit Slim's, Mia Wallace tells Vincent Vega about her fifteen minutes of fame when she starred in a television pilot, *Fox Force Five*, with four other "foxy chicks" who were also secret agents, each one "a force to be reckoned with." Uma's fox, Raven McCoy, was reared by circus performers and loved to deliver death with a knife. And since Tarantino's own fictional habitat was an enormous circus of subtexts, it made sense for him to talk with Uma about borrowing the same five foxes for another film, just as he'd talked about having Travolta and Michael Madsen appear in a prequel to *Pulp Fiction,* a film with both Vega brothers, Vincent and Vic (Mr. Blonde). But the five foxes remained a construction inside Tarantino's head, and he (and Miramax) found another project for Uma: an adaptation of Peter O'Donnell's *Modesty Blaise*.

Both a comic strip and an avalanche of books, *Modesty* featured a former queen of crime who now did favors for the British secret service; a Pop Art icon of the sixties (the strip began in 1963), she was a femme fatale who seemed like a perfect match for Tarantino's menagerie, so perfect that Vincent Vega "dies" on the toilet while reading *Modesty Blaise*. A six-year-old amnesiac, Modesty was found wandering all by herself in Greece; she became a shepherd, lived for a while in a refugee camp, managed to dance out from under a local brothel, had her own crime syndicate long before she was twenty, named herself after the mentor of Merlin the Magician: Blaise . . .

Tarantino wanted to start his own franchise, have different versions of *Modesty* directed by himself and members of a Miramax clan that included Robert Rodriguez, with Uma rivaling James Bond in film after film. But *Fox Force Five* and *Modesty Blaise* would morph into another project: *Kill Bill,* a revenge tale about a member of a killer elite who breaks away from her "handler," Bill, and is about to marry a local yokel in a small Texas town when Bill appears at the wedding rehearsal with the rest of his DiVAS (Deadly Viper Assassination Squad), who blow away everyone inside the chapel, including The Bride (Uma) and her unborn baby.

Yet according to Tarantino, The Bride had been brewing in him long before that, as he told Charlie Rose in 2004. He was sitting with Uma at a pub in Santa Monica, the Daily Pint, in the midst of shooting *Pulp Fiction* and mentioned his idea for a revenge movie, where Uma would be "the deadliest woman in the world." And in a revenge movie, "they always start with the person lying there," bloody and beaten-up, he said. Uma chipped in. " '[W]hat about you see me, my face, it's all bloody, and then the camera pans back, and you realize I'm in a bridal gown?' And that's where The Bride was born," with a little help from Modesty and Raven McCoy.

But Uma still had to wait as Tarantino went on to *Jackie Brown* and struggled with his World War II script; he would bump into Uma, who kept asking him about *Kill Bill,* so he took out the thirty pages of *Bill* that he'd begun, and "by taming *Kill Bill*, that would teach me to tame my war film," Tarantino thought.

"Once I got going, I just wrote and rewrote for a whole year. If I hit a snag I would just stop and watch a martial arts movie. I basically watched at least one Hong Kong movie a day, and sometimes two or three a day . . . I knew absolutely nothing about any of the Hollywood films that had been released during that year," Tarantino writes in the production notes to *Kill Bill*. He assembled his cast—Uma as The Bride, Warren Beatty as Bill, Michael Madsen as Bill's younger brother, Budd. He went to London to recruit Daryl Hannah as Elle Driver, aka California Mountain Snake, the one-eyed DiVA who has replaced The Bride in Bill's affections. Tarantino showed up backstage while Hannah was appearing in a revival of *The Seven Year Itch*, and told her that he'd written the part of Elle for her. Hannah didn't need much convincing. "I'd never played a full-out villain before, so I was really excited when I realized what a bad ass Elle Driver was." She had been a "bad ass" in Ridley Scott's *Blade Runner* (1982), where she plays Pris, the acrobatic android who nearly chokes Harrison Ford to death with the serpentine force of her long, long legs. But Elle is much more menacing and comic than Pris, who is programmed to be both a love doll and a killing machine. We're in Tarantinoland, and Elle

delivers her lines with the pungent flatness of a latter-day
W. C. Fields.

Startling as she is, Hannah's less of a revelation than Lucy
Liu as O-Ren Ishii, the halfbreed boss of Tokyo's underworld.
O-Ren dominates the first "volume" of *Bill*. She's the one
character with an unwavering narrative line; we see her as an
eight-year-old child watching the destruction of her parents
by an earlier crime lord; we watch her take revenge while
she's still a child; we sense the logic of her becoming a hired
assassin. Having been robbed of her own history, she lives in
that void where history has a hard time. She's a cinematic
ghost, like much of Tarantino's menagerie, and has remained
a child, with a child's grace and murderous dreams. But none
of this would matter unless Lucy Liu had "unlocked" O-Ren,
found her own way into the void. Tarantino had imagined
someone who was much more androgynous, but Lucy Liu *re-
imagined* O-Ren. "I like the idea of being very feminine, if
only on the surface. She is superficially very doll-like, not
what you would expect of a ruthless killer. This is a form of
camouflage for her. It puts her enemies off guard."

And us, too. We are also off guard. O-Ren is as funny,
cruel, and perverse as the Queen of Hearts. The Queen talks
of lopping off heads, and O-Ren does it. But her doll-like
manner is more than camouflage, more than a mask. It's the
revenge of a child on *all* adults. And it lulls her, keeps O-Ren

from going berserk—it's the ritualized language and lullaby that comes right out of the void . . .

Tarantino had assembled his cast. Call it late spring of 2001. We're at Cannes. Harvey Scissorhands had prepared to tell the entire film festival that *Bill* was about to go into production . . . when Tarantino told him that Uma Thurman was pregnant with her second child (at the time she was married to actor Ethan Hawke). The movie clock was ticking: sets had been built, a crew was hired. (The House of Blue Leaves, a restaurant and club that served as O-Ren's hangout and headquarters, had risen up like a two-story mountain *inside* the Beijing Film Studio, on one of the largest soundstages in the world). Warren Beatty thought that Uma should be replaced by Winona Ryder or Gwyneth Paltrow. But he hadn't tested Tarantino's stubbornness. *Kill Bill* was his Josef von Sternberg movie, he said. "If you're Josef von Sternberg, and you're about to start shooting *Morocco* in 1930, and Marlene Dietrich gets pregnant, what do you do? Do you go ahead and make the movie with someone else? Of course not. You wait for Dietrich."

Beatty himself was replaced by David Carradine, still known throughout the planet as Caine, a renegade monk who wandered the earth in *Kung Fu*—a cult television series of the seventies that would inspire Jules (Samuel L. Jackson) to give up killing people and wander the earth, "like Caine."

And Tarantino would later swear that Uma's pregnancy was almost a divine accident. "[W]e really needed the extra pre-production time. In the end I think Uma's son did us a favor." At least that's what he said in the production notes.

The baby was born in January 2002, and Uma arrived at the *Kill Bill* training center (a warehouse in Culver City) on March 2. The cast learned Japanese and studied samurai swordplay from Sonny Chiba, Tarantino's own idol, who had starred as a preachy assassin, Hattori Hanzo, in *Shadow Warriors*.

Cast and crew descended upon Beijing like a little army in May. The film studio had been built by Mao in 1949 as part of his propaganda machine. What appealed to Tarantino was the studio's utter insulation. "It is a complete village run by people whose job for life is to make movies."

It took eight weeks to shoot the 20-minute battle in the House of Blue Leaves, which was a scant two weeks less than it took to shoot the whole of *Pulp Fiction*. But the finale, a swordfight between The Bride and O-Ren in the Snow Garden, was worth the eight weeks—it has a beauty and a mathematical precision that we'd never seen before, not in Tarantino. The Bride scalps O-Ren with her magical sword, and we mourn this childlike queen of the under-world in a way that we can never mourn the other DiVAS. O-Ren has disturbed our psyche, O-Ren has ripped into the dream of the film. It's as if her death has robbed us of our own childhood, when we had to shove in and out of some void.

When Harvey Scissorhands himself showed up in China and saw the first half of *Kill Bill,* with the climactic fight in the Snow Garden, both he and Tarantino now realized that they had some sort of monster on their hands. "This is a terrific ending!" said Harvey. "So that's it! It's two movies."

2.

We open in the dark, listen to someone's labored breathing. Uma's bloodied face appears on the left side of the screen, an icon in black and white–beautiful and horrifying at the same instant. The icon overpowers us, and for a moment we're removed from the Technicolor world of cinema itself. Uma could be some suffering female Christ, and we can't be neutral. We're utterly involved in her pain.

This Christ doesn't need a cross; she's lying on the floor. The clack of someone's boots breaks through the sound of her breathing. A hand appears like a benevolent claw, clutching a white handkerchief with the monogram "Bill." Uma cringes at first, as if she's about to be attacked. Bill wipes the blood, almost apologizes. His silver bracelet seems to match the silver of her face. She shouldn't consider him a sadist, he says. "No, Kiddo, at this moment, this is me at my most sadistic."

We listen to him loading a shell.

"Bill," she says, "it's your baby."

A gun goes off; blood splatters from the side of her face, splatters onto the floor . . . and the gown she's wearing.

We move into the dark again, the film's titles running in white letters on a black field, while Nancy Sinatra sings "(Bang Bang) My Baby Shot Me Down." And this song about betrayal, about love lost, love shot down, teases us *and* serves as some kind of sing-along to that short, brutal ballad surrounding Uma's bloody face. The black of the screen turns into a silhouette of Uma in profile, Uma lying down, the contours of her face like a series of cliffs . . .

The next scene is ruinous. And it's the film's first chapter, entitled "2" with a circle drawn around it, as if it were part of some list we haven't seen. Black and white are gone; we're in a land of pastel colors. Uma drives up to some picture-book cottage in Pasadena that could be a dollhouse. She's come in a yellow pickup truck, wearing a leather jacket and jeans. We've lost all the earlier iconography of a female Christ. The dollhouse lawn is covered with toys. Uma rings the doorbell with a long, double-jointed finger. Vivica A. Fox opens the door. They start to fight. Tarantino tries to explain himself in the production notes. In the world of *Kill Bill,* "women are not the weaker sex. They have exactly the same predatory hunting instincts as the men, the same drive to kill or be killed."

I still had a hard time to keep from laughing when the two Amazons battle it out with a frying pan and a kitchen knife. But at least we learn who the Amazons are. They're both ex-Vipers who belonged to Bill. Currently a Pasadena housewife known as Jeanie Bell, Vivica was once Vernita Green, aka Copperhead, and Uma herself was Black Mamba. Vernita has a four-year-old child, Nikki, who interrupts the Amazons when she comes home from school and sees signs of battle strewn all over the house, such as giant green crystals of shattered glass. Nikki is sent to her room. The two Amazons have coffee in the kitchen, and their dialogue seems as if it had come right out of *Fox Force Five*, Mia Wallace's doomed television pilot in *Pulp Fiction*.

"I know I fucked you over, I fucked you over bad," says Vernita, Bill's one black Viper, who feels *she* should have been called Black Mamba . . . and tries to kill the false Black Mamba with a gun hidden in a box of cereal. But she misses, and Black Mamba hurls a hunting knife into the middle of Vernita's chest, just like Raven McCoy, the knife-throwing assassin of *Fox Force Five*, would have done.

Nikki comes into the kitchen and sees her dead mother lying on the floor.

And Black Mamba begins to sound like John Wayne. "When you grow up, if you're still raw about it, I'll be waitin'."

Tarantino has even talked of a sequel to *Kill Bill,* when in fifteen years or so, Nikki, now a ninja, will battle it out with Black Mamba. But sequel or not, we can't be sure of how to react to the confrontation between Black Mamba and the little girl, whether to laugh, cry, or have a nervous giggle. It's impossible to read Tarantino's intentions, or the tone of this scene. Vernita's death is out of sequence. She's the second one on Black Mamba's kill list (hence the "two" of the chapter title). A. O. Scott, chief film critic at the *New York Times,* believes that this "may be a tongue-in-cheek nod to a venerable Hollywood convention: the black character dies first."

Even if it is totally tongue-in-cheek, a slap at Hollywood itself, the scene still feels out of joint, as if Tarantino's sense of form has abandoned him for a moment, and his dialogue, so often funny and perverse as it rips away at all our precious artifacts, has become one more piece of junk.

"Sentence first—verdict afterwards," says the Queen of Hearts, who could be reigning over *Kill Bill*. "Answers first, questions later," Tarantino loves to say about his own films. "[N]o flashbacks, just chapters. But in America, movies have got to be linear: if you begin a scene at the beginning of a

race, you have to end it at the end of the race." And Tarantino wants to drop us right into the *middle*. Black Mamba
defending herself with a frying pan may be a savage shift
from the fallen icon with blood on her face, but it isn't savage
enough—it's silly. It takes us into a cartoon world a little too
soon, and it's a bad cartoon, drowning in thick candy colors
and sentimental talk.

But the film recovers right after Black Mamba rides away
in her "Pussy Wagon," which she stole from a hospital
orderly who had been using her as a sexual machine.
Chapter Two ("The Blood-Splattered Bride") returns us to the
rural wedding chapel where Black Mamba had been shot in
the head by Bill and continues the chronology. This time
there are no picture-book cottages, just a load of tumbleweed.
Michael Parks, another actor Tarantino has rescued from
oblivion, plays a local sheriff with dumb, demonic brilliance.
The camera picks up details with an artist's eye: from the row
of sunglasses on the sheriff's dashboard to the cops and
corpses inside the chapel, like a cluster of flowers with Black
Mamba in the middle, lying on the floor with a swollen belly
. . . and blood on her bridal gown. Parks is a Texas Charlie
Chan with his own "Son Number One," who serves as his
deputy and who dubs Black Mamba "The Bride." The sheriff
has a distinctive tone and voice that Vernita Green never has.
He surveys the carnage in his sunglasses and says, "A sure

and steady hand did this. This ain't the work of a squirrelly amateur . . . If you was a moron you could almost admire it." The Bride becomes an icon again in the sheriff's gaze, tinted green through the miracle of his sunglasses.

He removes his sunglasses, and now The Bride's face is lit in her own blood.

"She was a blood-splattered angel," he says, just before The Bride coughs (or spits) blood in his eye. The sheriff squints. "Son Number One, this tall . . . cocksucker ain't dead." And we're back in Tarantino country, where the absurd mixes with the macabre, where the dialogue sings, where death and mutilation have their own gorgeous design.

Next we're in a hospital room, where The Bride is lying in a coma, her face lit like an icon in blue. Elle Driver enters, wearing a nurse's uniform, with a red cross on her eye patch. She's about to "deliver" The Bride with a dose of poison when her cell phone rings. It's Bill. He tells her to abort the mission. He won't have Black Mamba killed while she's comatose. "We've done a lot of things to this lady, and if she ever wakes up we'll do a whole lot more."

While Bill is in the midst of a lover's spat with Elle, the camera blinks and cuts to an image of Bill's hand, caressing the black hilt of a samurai sword. That hand is the most menacing device in the film: it caresses and kills, caresses and kills. And Bill is the film's American Fu Manchu, who seems to catch us off guard and lull us to sleep with his disembodied voice . . .

Four years pass. The Bride continues to lie in a coma. A mosquito lands on her skin and sucks at her blood. She wakes up with a jolt . . . like the bride of Frankenstein. She taps the metal plate in her skull, feels the scars on her stomach, mourns the baby she thinks she's lost. But she can't afford to cry. One of the orderlies has been renting her out while she was comatose. And in a scene that reminds us of the pawnshop and the two sodomizing rednecks in *Pulp Fiction,* The Bride gets rid of the orderly and the redneck who has paid to hump her. She's become a killer again.

The Bride goes to Okinawa, persuades Hattori Hanzo (Sonny Chiba), the last of the great samurai swordsmiths, to come out of retirement and craft her a weapon so that she can kill Bill, one of his former pupils. Hattori realizes that this is his "finest sword." He tells The Bride: "If on your journey you should encounter God . . . God will be cut."

She takes her sword to Tokyo and the House of Blue Leaves, challenges O-Ren and her "powerful posse, The Crazy 88," lops off the arm of her lawyer and best friend, Sofie Fatale (Julie Dreyfus), duels with Gogo Yubari (Chiaki Kuriyama), O-Ren's teenybopper bodyguard, and has to use her own Hattori Hanzo against the entire "88," who are dressed in black suits like the Reservoir Dogs and wear the same black masks that Bruce Lee wore in *The Green Hornet.*

This long, long battle is the most problematic part of the film. A. O. Scott compares it to "a show-stopping musical number," which Tarantino meant it to be. But it's also a study in excess, and feels closer to Mack Sennett's Keystone Kops than to the maneuvers of samurai swordplay. The mayhem goes on and on, as it did with the Kops, whose motions became more and more convoluted, sucking more and more people in, until "a whole city, an entire civilization" seems involved in the destruction. Of course, the Kops used cotton billy clubs, and their worst bangs didn't even leave a bump, and Tarantino litters the House of Blue Leaves with "severed limbs and writhing trunks." Yet we don't seem to cringe the way we did when Mr. Blonde lops off Marvin's ear in *Reservoir Dogs.* There's a sense of play about the sword fights, and we know that The Bride will never be harmed, even if Gogo nearly rips her apart with her barbed iron ball.

The House of Blue Leaves is another of Tarantino's caverns, like Jack Rabbit Slim's, a cave where we come for respite from the routines of everyday life, and where Tarantino situates his cinema. It's another wax museum with a pulse rate . . . or some kind of cartoon factory, like Warner Bros.' answer to Donald Duck and Mickey Mouse—*Looney Tunes*, which was much more anarchic than Disney's animal farm and where severed heads or limbs could fly across the landscape, pursued by Bugs Bunny or Daffy Duck.

The Bride spanks one of the "88," a wisp of a boy. "This is what you get for fucking around with yakuzas. Go home to your mother." And she returns to the carnage, leaving more severed heads and limbs.

3.

Finally there's the fight in the snow, which is outside the realm of *Looney Tunes* or the comic mischief of the earlier battles. O-Ren is "lifted" from the heroine of *Lady Snowblood* (1973), a female samurai epic about a woman in a white kimono who avenges the death of her family; O-Ren also wears a white kimono at the House of Blue Leaves, also avenges the death of her mother and father; but unlike Lady Snowblood, she watched them die. Her fight with Black Mamba isn't the least bit cartoonish; yet she's born out of a cartoon. We first meet O-Ren in Tarantino's eight-minute anime, the most electrifying and original piece of *Kill Bill;* it's manga seen through the eyes of a movie maniac. O-Ren hides under a bed while her father battles the minions of Boss Matsimoto; this little cartoon is much bloodier than the rest of the film—it's filled with red rain—and much more intimate. We're under the bed with O-Ren, breathing in the carnage, which isn't nearly as ritualized as the carnage in the House of Blue Leaves. And O-Ren has remained that eight-year-old girl, frozen into a dream of blood.

After she wounds Black Mamba in the snow, she pouts like a petulant child and says with a naughty smile: "Silly Caucasian girl likes to play with samurai swords." O-Ren is no ordinary Amazon; she's the fury who comes out of the void.

The most frightening moment in the film occurs at the very end of the anime. We've watched O-Ren grow up into one of Bill's best female assassins (he will help her become Tokyo's crime lord); but here O-Ren and the other Vipers attack Black Mamba inside the chapel; they stand in a circle and punch at her, and she buffets from blow to blow, her bridal veil billowing around her as O-Ren delivers the coup de grace, a kick that sends her tumbling to the floor. This is how we will find her at the beginning of *Kill Bill*, with blood on her face . . .

And now she's in the Snow Garden, wearing a yellow jumpsuit like the one Bruce Lee wore in his last film, *Game of Death* (released long after he died and rendering him the ghost of a ghost on our screens). But The Bride is much less of a ghost than Bruce Lee. And her swordfight with O-Ren, the entire episode in the garden, has a lyric sense of detail that we've rarely seen in Tarantino. There are no rough edges in this garden, no gargoyles in the background to plague us or oblige us to laugh, not a single groan of yakuzas who've lost their limbs. O-Ren and The Bride fight to flamenco music; Tarantino claims that this is what inspired him; he had the flamenco music "before I wrote the scene," according to the production notes. "It's the music that helps me find the rhythm of the movie, the beat the movie will play."

But there's another sound that dominates the scene, a sound that's almost as silent as snow itself, *or* that disturbs the silence of the snow; and the flamenco music drowns it, drives it away. We first hear it when The Bride enters the garden; it's a soft thump that's hard to define. We cannot see its source; we hear this thump every fifteen seconds or so, until the fight begins, and then it goes away . . . and returns after O-Ren herself is wounded. Suddenly we can see a curious instrument, a kind of fake little fountain that none of us would ever have noticed unless we'd been to such a garden. It's called *shishi-odoshi,* or "scarestag"—that is, a rhythmic, reverberating scarecrow, placed near a forest to frighten animals away with its repeated thumps. The "scarestag" is visually striking because of its bamboo ladle, which slowly fills with water, then drops, hits a stone, and springs up again.

The ladle appears three times during the duel, like a signal of O-Ren's unraveling, and the sound of her own quiet doom. It also acts as a hinge on the left side of the frame, a magical semaphore that enthralls us with its unfamiliar motion. It takes us outside the landscape of comic books—cartoon battles, assassination squads, masked yakuzas—and into a beauty that's like the longing of language itself, as if Tarantino were recognizing for a moment that there was something beyond his reach . . .

4.

His meditation doesn't last. We return to the intrigue. The Bride rolls Sofie Fatale and her one remaining arm down a hill to a hospital emergency room as a message to Bill. That's the reason Sofie is still alive: she can tell Bill of the carnage in the House of Blue Leaves. The Bride is coming to kill Bill . . .

Next we have another icon: Sofie Fatale, her face tinted blue as it would be in a sinister comic book. We see Bill's hand and an IV tube, both of them also blue. Sofie seems to be in a hospital. Bill soothes her with his disembodied voice. "Sofie, Sofie, my Sofie . . . my beautiful and brilliant Sofie." He strokes her with his right hand, the very same claw that wiped the blood off Black Mamba's face . . . moments before she was shot in the head. We don't quite know how to relate to this hand, which can be tender and full of tricks. It's all of Bill we ever see in *Kill Bill Vol. 1*. He controls events from afar, ordering Elle not to kill The Bride while she's still in a coma. But The Bride is out of control, on a rampage, and the real power of *Vol. 1* is that Bill is always in the background, a puppeteer whose only presence is his claw of a hand, his boots, and his baritone . . .

Vol. 2 is another matter. Fu Manchu becomes a spurned lover—and martial arts move into domestic comedy. "David [Carradine] dominates *Vol. 2*," according to Tarantino. He appears in the very first scene, making his entrance with a flute. He's waiting for Black Mamba outside the wedding chapel. Tarantino relives for us the events just prior to the "Massacre at Two Pines."

"I mean, this scene just sings. The crew got choked up watching," says Carradine in the production notes. "Quentin came over to me and said: 'I think this is the best scene in the picture for you.' And I said, " 'I think it's the best scene of my career.' "

It's also the scene that nearly sinks the entire enterprise. Tarantino likes to consider the various influences on *Bill*. "If my life had two sides, one side would be the Shaw Brothers [and their martial arts pictures made in Hong Kong], and the other side would be Italian Westerns." But the scene on the chapel porch has less to do with Sergio Leone or the action directors of Hong Kong than with Douglas Sirk, *bad* Douglas Sirk, at the edge of silliness and hardcore melodrama. Tarantino reverses his aesthetic principle of "questions first, answers later" in *Kill Bill.* He says *Vol. 1* asks the questions, and *Vol. 2* gives the answers. But the answers are already *inside* the questions, as he ought to know. And suddenly the teacher becomes his own worst pupil. The cameo at Two Pines should have remained on the cutting-room floor. By attempting to "humanize" the massacre, he weakens its force.

Bill has come to kill The Bride with his own special kiss.

"Are you gonna be nice?" she asks.

"I've never been nice in my whole life, but I'll do my best to be sweet."

But there's no "heat" in this scene, and nothing much really passes between them. "Bill is a pimp," according to Tarantino. "He's a procurer in every way, except for him it's about death, murder, and killing as opposed to sex." But we need *something* sexual on the porch at Two Pines, to feel Bill's jealous rage . . . and all we get is a deadpan delivery and a deadpan face. Carradine was better in the background. He's a terrific Fu Manchu; he still walks the earth with his own serious weight and without a sense of humor, like Caine in *Kung Fu.*

Tarantino wrote Bill's lines with Samuel L. Jackson's voice and rhythms in his head, though he knew that Jackson would never play the part. It's a pity. Jackson could have played Bill, so could John Travolta, or Christopher Walken, but the role should have gone to Warren Beatty. Beatty would have been a perfect Bill—an aging pimp who could reveal much, much more in his eyes. Beatty would have "toyed" with Black Mamba, teased her, while delivering the very same lines. But with all his charm, he couldn't have saved the scene. It's filler material—flotsam—rather than backstory. If Tarantino's original idea was about "an assassin who tries to leave the business," then the backstory should have been about this business.

"There are no good guys in a Tarantino movie," according to David Carradine. "It's *all* about the bad guys [and girls]. The essence of a Tarantino movie is an inside look at the minds and hearts of violent people." And we're curious about these badasses, and about Black Mamba's life as a DiVA. The funniest moment in the film is a flashback— Beatrix Kiddo (The Bride's real name) is trying to tell Bill why she ran away from him and the Deadly Vipers: she's in a hotel room in LA, sent to kill a certain Lisa Wong. But she felt sick even before she got on the plane. And we watch her administer a ninety-second pregnancy test; a strip filled with her urine turns blue. "Fuck," she says. Her doorbell rings—Lisa Wong has sent her own assassin, Karen Kim, who blasts a hole in the door; Beatrix does a somersault and lands behind her bed, gun in hand. There's a Mexican standoff. "I'm a fuckin' surgeon with this shotgun," the assassin says.

And Beatrix answers: "Guess what, bitch? I'm better than Annie Oakley and I got you in my sight." Beatrix insists she found out she was pregnant a moment before Karen shot a hole in the door. The assassin doesn't believe her. "I'm the deadliest woman in the world," Beatrix says, "but right now I'm just scared shitless for my baby. Please!"

Karen sits down on the floor with her shotgun and examines the blue strip. "I don't know what this fuckin' shit means." She starts to read the instructions; a truce is declared. Beatrix promises never to go after Lisa Wong. The last image we have is of Karen's face in the halo that her shotgun has left in the door. "Congratulations!" she says.

The flashback is absurd and insane, like a marvelous comic strip, touching us while it makes us laugh. Comics are the key to *Kill Bill*–a comic-book world drives the narrative, carries the motifs. The film seems to move from panel to panel as it meditates on the notion of the superhero, whether it's an actual comic book revealing the bloody origins of O-Ren, or The Bride delivering herself from her own grave, like the sturdiest of superheroes.

If The Bride's antics aren't enough evidence, Bill lectures to us on "the mythology around superheroes," as if he were some instructor in a freshman sociology class and we were his witless pupils. "As you know," he tells The Bride, "I'm quite keen on comic books," but he's really talking to us. Superman, he says, is not a great comic book, but "the mythology is unique," particularly the relationship between the hero and his alter ego. Peter Parker has to put on a costume to become Spider-Man, but "when Superman wakes up in the morning he's Superman." Clark Kent is the costume he wears to blend in with us. "Clark Kent is Superman's critique on the whole human race. Clark Kent is how Superman views us"—four-eyed and feeble. And Bill likens The Bride, Beatrix Kiddo, to Superman wearing the costume of Clark Kent.

"Are you calling me a superhero?" she asks.

"I'm calling you a killer," a killer who attempted to disguise herself as a worker bee at Two Pines. The wedding veil was her costume. "You're a renegade killer bee, not a worker bee."

The whole Superman riff is ludicrous. Tarantino seems to have lost his savage sense of humor; he's preaching to us, trying to sound serious, and there's no one on the set—not Harvey Scissorhands, not Lawrence Bender, not Beatrix Kiddo—to tell him he's full of baloney.

Tarantino buffs may like this "humanizing" of Bill, his little sermon, his appearance with B.B., the four-year-old daughter Beatrix thought had died in her womb. Bill, aka Snake Charmer, a killer and trainer of killer bees, suddenly wears the costume and cloak of the good father at his Mexican hacienda-hideout. He makes a sandwich for B.B., cuts off the crusts, tells her that he's been bad to "Mommy," that he grew forlorn after shooting her in the head.

Tarantino expects us to buy the legend of Bill as the abandoned "husband," so in love with Beatrix Kiddo that he lost his cool. The film's other male characters support this legend. Bill's estranged brother, Budd (Michael Madsen) says to Elle: "I never saw anyone buffalo Bill the way she [Beatrix] buffaloed Bill." And he buries Beatrix alive—"for breakin' my brother's heart."

Bill is an orphan who never saw his own dad. He was raised in a Mexican brothel by Esteban, an eighty-year-old pimp (Michael Parks) who tells Beatrix he took Bill as a little boy to see *The Postman Always Rings Twice* (1946), with John Garfield as the witless hero and Lana Turner as the big bad blonde who destroys him. Bill couldn't stop crying. "This boy was a fool for blondes," says Esteban, looking at Beatrix, another blonde. Esteban says he never would have shot Beatrix in the head. He would only have cut her face . . . and put her back in his harem.

Uma also suffers from Bill's little streak of humanity. Her challenge as an actress was to find "the human inside this unreal, insane, mad epic," according to the production notes. But it's this *humanity* that kills *Kill Bill,* slows the film, weighs it down, punctures its macabre energy. Do we have to watch Budd's own Stations of the Cross, his suffering as a bouncer at a "titty bar," a fallen DiVA who has to clean out the crap in the toilet?

Vol. 2 is unbearable until Budd shoots Beatrix in the chest
with a double dose of rock salt and buries her with a flashlight
so she won't have to die in the dark. Now the fun begins.
Budd offers to sell The Bride's Hattori Hanzo sword to Elle
Driver for a million bucks. Elle brings the million to Budd's
trailer, with a black mamba hidden in the money bag, a
mamba that bites him in the face, and while he writhes on the
floor she reads him a little treatise on the mamba's venom
that she got off the Internet.

Black Mamba breaks through the door—a human snake
who broke out of her tomb with a trick from her master, Pai
Mei, the monk with white eyebrows. "I wanted it to be the
ultimate cinematic cat fight of all time," says Tarantino, and it
is. The Bride could be dueling with her own demonic double
. . . a double right out of Superman.

With all his preaching and his love of comic books, Bill
never got to complete Superman's mythology. The Man of
Steel has his own double—an imitation Superman called
Bizarro, the Thing of Steel, with tangled hair, chalky skin,
and speech that sounds like a dull, ungrammatical Queen of
Hearts. With his own dim bride, Bizarro-Lois, he rules Htrae,
"the strangest, whackiest planet in the universe . . . the square
Bizarro world."

This boxlike planet is overrun with ghostly doubles of
Superman, Superboy, and Lois Lane. To set himself off from

all the other hapless Supermen, Bizarro wears a medallion that establishes his identity as "Bizarro No. 1." But he's doomed to doing everything ass-backward. "The Bizarro world is a mad version of everything earthly," where no means yes, bad means good, ugly is better than beautiful, and dull is the greatest compliment Superman can give.

Bizarro's creator, Lex Luthor, is a renegade scientist and Superman's nemesis; he's also a cruel jokester, having built Bizarro out of *nothing,* as all creators must do. And Tarantino is some kind of Lex Luthor, constructing a madcap world in *Kill Bill* that bounces off our own, and is most affecting the more monstrous it is, as when Tokyo's queen of crime stands on the table of her crime council and tells the other bosses in the sweet tones of a geisha that "no subject will ever be taboo," but the price they pay for mentioning her own mongrel heritage is—"I collect your fucking head."

Tarantino has mastered a savage landscape that pays homage to every form of film—noir, spaghetti western, musical, romantic comedy, blaxploitation, samurai adventure, animation, kung fu epic—by swallowing it whole and spitting it back at us in a manner we've never seen before. The "wirework" of martial arts choreographer Yuen Wo-Ping is not as spectacular as it is in *Crouching Tiger, Hidden Dragon* (2000), where women warriors sail along the rooftops, catapulted by wires that are "erased" from the screen. There are plenty of wires in the House of Blue Leaves, but we have Yuen Wo-Ping's choreography according to Quentin Tarantino—funnier, more grotesque. His cruelty often has a tender tug, and is much more intimate than when Tarantino's adults try to talk like adults, as in "The Final Chapter: Face To Face," with Bill and Beatrix, and B.B. in the middle. When his adults aren't wailing or screaming like infants, they have little to say, and if they speak, they sermonize on Superman. Their affection—the tenderness—comes after a fight. Bill and Beatrix have a short duel while they're sitting down, and then she pokes him in the chest. It's fatal, the "five-point-palm exploding heart technique," taught to her by Pai Mei—the deadliest blow in all of martial arts, as Bill himself had once explained to Beatrix. The master "hits you with his fingertips at five different pressure points on your body and then lets you walk away . . . and once you've taken five steps your heart explodes inside your body."

Beatrix was Pai Mei's best pupil, not Bill. Pai Mei never revealed that mystery to him. Once poked in the chest, Bill starts to bleed. Beatrix holds his hand. It's a little like love-making. He takes his five steps (actually six) and drops dead.

Therein lies the problem of the film. In a Bizarro world, the five-point-palm exploding heart technique wouldn't kill Bill. Bill should have survived . . . if only Tarantino had kept his "wild way." Or maybe I miss the roller-coaster ride of

Pulp Fiction, and prefer it to a showdown in Mexico that's predictable from miles and miles away.

Note: There are endless references, endless reverberations, as Tarantino—a full-grown Alice—takes us through the Looking Glass. We might begin with "Beatrix." The name is too unusual *not* to refer back to Beatrix Potter, author of the Peter Rabbit books. Rabbits abound in Tarantinoland. After Beatrix, aka The Bride, kills Gogo in *Vol. 1,* O-Ren stands on the balcony of the House of Blue Leaves as her reinforcements arrive. She smiles at Beatrix, who thought that her next battle was going to be with O-Ren. "Silly rabbit," she says. Beatrix continues the mantra: "Trix are for . . ." And O-Ren joins in: ". . . kids," as if they were co-conspirators in a world where children rule. They're reciting the totem words of Trix, a puffed corn cereal "with the natural taste of fruit." In TV commercials the Trix rabbit—big, white, with enormous floppy ears—would try to swipe the fruity balls of cereal. And two kids, a boy and a girl, the guardians of Trix, would catch the rabbit before he could get into the bowl. "Silly rabbit, Trix are for kids." Tarantino, a cereal freak, must have grown up with the Trix rabbit, who was "born" in 1960, three years before Tarantino himself. . . .

finale

The Anchovy Bandit

1.

Picture a boy of five. Probably sitting in the dark while he watches images float along a white wall. And if he's from some heartland like the Bronx, or one of the beach towns at the border of LA, those images will thicken his blood, seem more solid to him than his very own skin. Perhaps it wasn't so vital for a girl-child, who had her own collection of dolls and wouldn't have wandered into the anomie of a moviehouse (not if she was from the Bronx), but for a man-child like me movies made all the difference.

Movies taught me how to kiss, how to hold a knife and fork, how to talk like Cary Grant, how to die with my boots on, like Errol Flynn pretending to be someone named Custer. Errol Flynn's demise at the hands of the Sioux was intolerable, but at least Errol had his sword and his six-gun, his bugler right behind him, but how could *any* child, boy or girl, recover from the destruction of Bambi's mom by a monster known as He?

Even at five I was no fool. *He* represented those adults who
trampled on the grass, upset the magic bounty of the forest,
made an orphan of deer and rabbit cubs, and would have
driven human cubs from the moviehouse. No adult could be
trusted, except for the old Prince who had sired Bambi, but
the old Prince didn't count, since animals were hardly better
than children. And so there was a strange complicity between
the forest animals and ourselves. Not only Bambi and Faline,
but Dumbo and Donald Duck . . . and Popeye, since cartoon
characters were also like children living in a barnyard with
other "toons"—marvelous and monstrous because they could
sound like adults, wear what adults would wear, but could
never graduate to genuine adulthood.

How could we know that sitting in our seats we'd stumbled
upon the trappings of our patriarchal culture, a culture that
kept us small, that distrusted whatever was feminine or
instinctual, that would have gone on killing Bambi's mother
till the end of time? Of course the "adults" on our white wall—
Errol Flynn or Veronica Lake—had the tantrums and tem-
perament of children, and the profound narcissism of
children who loved being watched by a million people, and
would change roles with all the caprice of buying a new hat.

And we ourselves soon discovered comic books—compan-
ions to whatever we saw on the screen. Comics taught me
how to read in better fashion than any kindergarten or first

grade ever could. Kindergarten didn't have panels and balloons with words inside, like Holy Moley or Shazam. Kindergarten didn't have Captain Marvel, who was much dearer to me than Superman. Marvel wasn't a big lug. He was a boy named Billy Batson, who could have come from Westchester or another suburb of the Bronx. Billy had his own lavish chemistry set and radio station to help him thwart Dr. Sivana, a wicked genius who looked like a wizened prune with big ears and powerful glasses—that face of his has haunted me for sixty years.

A boy with a chemistry set was no match for Dr. Sivana and a dust ray that could tear through skin and turn grocers and bankers into the tiniest speck. He had to call upon his "other form," Captain Marvel, who was a stronger, idealized version of himself—that is, a boy masquerading as an adult, imagining the powers that an adult might have. Captain Marvel was like Billy's own magical erection, summoned with the secret word "Shazam!" And "the world's mightiest mortal" would catch up with "the world's maddest scientist" on his rocket ship . . . and the wizened prune would begin to cower.

"Have pity on a weak old man!"

It was only a trick. Sivana would shove a gadget into Marvel's mouth that made him mouth "Shazam!" and reduced him back to Billy Batson. But it hardly mattered.

Silvana himself was a child. He, Marvel, and Billy were all in the same boat–children, naughty or otherwise, who would never become bankers or grocers, never give in to the trappings or tricks of adults . . .

I'm not tyrannizing Tarantino, imposing my own childhood upon him, but I wonder if he didn't go through many of the same rituals. In dissecting *Kill Bill,* A. O. Scott says that Tarantino "has immersed himself, his characters and his audience in a highly artificial world, a looking-glass universe that reflects nothing beyond his own cinematic obsessions"–and comic-book obsessions, since Tarantino grew up with comics as much as he did with films. "Well, along with movies I'm a comic-book geek," he told Michel Ciment and Hubert Niogret of *Positif.* But his own reading of *Kill Bill* is quite schematic.

"I have said many times that there are two different worlds that my movies take place in," he confessed in the film's production notes. "One of them is the 'Quentin Universe' of *Pulp Fiction* and *Jackie Brown*–it's heightened but more or less realistic. The other is the Movie World. When characters in the Quentin Universe go to the movies, the stuff they see takes place in the Movie World. They act as a window into that world. *Kill Bill* is the first film I've made that takes place in the Movie World. This is me imagining what would happen if that world really existed, and I could take a film crew in there and make a Quentin Tarantino movie about those characters."

It sounds plausible, but it's not true. There's no great divide between *Pulp Fiction* and *Kill Bill*. Each of Tarantino's four films has a similar dynamic, a similar drive. Each is a child's look at an adult world, with a child's obsessions. *Reservoir Dogs* remains appealing not because it's a gangster film, but because *his* gangsters are closer to goblins than anything else. They bark at us, they bite. Sometimes they manage to kill people, but mostly they yak our heads off, just as Beatrix and Lisa Wong (the assassin sent to kill her) yak at each other with murderous weapons in their hands. And if Beatrix demolishes the Crazy 88 at the House of Blue Leaves, we don't really mourn them and their missing limbs, since their deaths are part of some fairy tale.

Tarantino's films, every single one, are about lovable and not so lovable monsters. This is his Movie World. "Few things are sadder than the truly monstrous," writes Nathanael West in *The Day of the Locust,* a novel about Hollywood gargoyles and goblins. But West's goblins are as funny as they are sad, and so are Tarantino's. Captain Koons with his scatological tale about a wandering watch; O-Ren with her kitten-like voice and raucous obscenities; Mr. Blonde with his mad, dancing razor; Jackie Brown on her conveyor belt, like some strange icon out of the '70s, a mythological movie monster;

Pumpkin and Honey Bunny, gremlins cooing at one another while they commit highway robbery in a restaurant; even Bill, the philosophical Fu Manchu, keen on comic books—they're all characters out of Tarantino's endless children's book, monsters in their own measure, living in an upside-down world, put in place to delight, scare, and enthrall.

John Travolta best articulates the dangers of this upside-down world. After dancing the twist with Uma Thurman at Jack Rabbit Slim's, drowning in the "fauna" of the 1950s, he has a nightmare. "I dreamed we had finished shooting at Jack Rabbit Slim's, and everyone went home except me, and I'm left there with all the other icons."

It's a child's dream of abandonment, of being lost among the icons, the icon he himself has become. Tarantino's decor is treacherous, full of traps, like some landscape in the mind of a witch.

2.

Bambi broke his heart; it was one of the first films he'd ever seen, together with *Carnal Knowledge* (1971), Mike Nichols' film about a couple of Peter Pans caught in their own juvenile fantasies. Tarantino himself seems stuck between *Bambi* and *Carnal Knowledge*. He had to run out of the theater when Bambi's mother died; it marked him as a moviegoer, and froze his sensibility in some crucial way. He's been a griever ever since, mourning Bambi's mom while he's made his films; and his mission has been to turn the "mother" into a kind of goddess who could bring herself back to life, like Beatrix Kiddo, who rises out of a coma and can only end her carnage *after* she's reunited with her lost child. In fact, Tarantino's films are about perplexed, parentless children who are stalled, who can't seem to start their own family.

Even if they do start a family with the help of some wayward miracle or magic wand, they're just as parentless—and just as virginal. The most virginal moment in all of Tarantino is the showdown between Bill and The Bride. They don't behave like former lovers, or like lovers at all. Perhaps Freudian scholars will read this scene as a confrontation between Tarantino (disguised as a female warrior) and his own lost father. I do not. Their aborted duel might be interpreted as a kiss. They're both like brutal children trying to be civilized in front of their own child, B.B., who's already a little actress utterly removed from her parents' strange struggle. I have a feeling she could have gone away with the gardener, continued her game of charades, while Mommy and Daddy lay dying or dead inside the hacienda . . .

Children are the only real seducers in Tarantino's menagerie. They have enormous eyes, like B.B., while Tarantino's adults are stunted children who have forgotten how to seduce. His women are Amazons who have little need of male company, and his men are starved of love, like murderous monks . . . or wounded Peter Pans.

If you watch him on the tube, chatting with martial-arts movie star, Jet Li, he looks like a rumpled giant, with all the enthusiasms of a boy—a Bizarro Huckleberry Finn, a teller of tall tales but without Huck's deep, deep sympathies (except for cutthroats). The *London Telegraph* insists that he has "the desperate air of a dorky white boy who wants to be black." I'd rather not get into the controversy of how many times he uses the word "nigger" in *Reservoir Dogs, Pulp Fiction,* or *Jackie Brown*. But he isn't Peter Pan in blackface. He mimics whites as much as he mimics blacks. He's cursed with his own kind of echolalia. Awash in various idiolects, he plays with the *music* of white and black gangster talk, like a child making mud pies in the sand.

His very first screenplay, *Captain Peachfuzz and the Anchovy Bandit,* written when he was fourteen, featured a man who robs pizza parlors, and this Anchovy Bandit could have been Tarantino himself, a boy relishing in lawlessness. His subject hasn't really changed that much—all his subsequent screenplays have been about criminals and their crimes.

Tarantino seems obsessed with assassins, but *his* assassins pout and pontificate, like Peter Pan. They're children with a cruel streak—murderous and funny—who take revenge on the "evil empire" of adults. This narrow focus has always been his strength. "His films have a heartbeat in a Hollywood that makes soulless pictures," according to director Bill Lustig–his films are personal and eccentric, rough and wild, and often ragged, the way Scorsese and Godard were once rough and ragged.

Mr. Blonde, Vincent, Jules, Bill, and The Bride are descendants of Travis Bickle, the sad-eyed, almost silent sociopath in Scorsese's *Taxi Driver.* Travis is a sympathetic monster who never learned to scream, a Frankenstein who looks in the mirror and sees an unsympathetic face. Tarantino's monsters howl at each other and love what they see in the mirror–a child looking at another child. But they're so removed from their feelings that they can hardly recognize their own pain . . . unless they happen to be shot in the head. They're monomaniacs on a particular quest, whether it's Jules after his "religious conversion," or The Bride seeking revenge. Their animus and their energy seem to come right out of the comic book, where a landscape, forever flattened, lends itself to monomania.

The disruptive energy that Tarantino revealed in the classroom, that kept him from sitting still as a second-grader, serves him well on screen–we can feel that hyperkinetic pull in every frame, as if we were living inside a comic-book panel filled with a child's exclamation marks. That's his signature, a need, almost a madness, to give pleasure moment by moment.

He wants to deliver a film that gets in your face . . . and stays in your face. But this hyperactivity doesn't work when he's acting instead of directing, where he tires us after a minute or two. His best performance is in *Pulp Fiction* as Jimmie of Toluca Lake, because he has John Travolta, Samuel L. Jackson, and Harvey Keitel to hold him in orbit. He was also wearing his own bathrobe, which was like a totem—a toy that soothed him, calmed his down. "I ate. I drank. I masturbated in that bathrobe." But without that strange "wire" in him, that terrible hunger to mix it up with his own actors, perform with them, become part of *their* menagerie, he might not have been able to give his actors the courage to sit on their own live wire, as Pam Grier did, ripping into the icon of Foxy Brown to reveal the terror and isolation inside herself.

"I get a chance to be both an actor and a director. As an actor I get to play all the characters," whether Bill or Jackie Brown. "You have heard of method acting. I am a method writer. I become the character as I am writing them . . . I am everybody." He was Ordell for a whole year, while writing *Jackie Brown.* "I had to really work hard in letting go of Ordell and letting Sam [Jackson] play him and not being a jerk about stuff. Sam was him for ten weeks. I was Ordell for fifty-two weeks."

And sometimes it really hurts. "[I]f I didn't act in *Jackie Brown,* you better believe I wanted to, that I was having a poison-ivy acting reaction! I was itching for it the entire time! When I was directing Robert De Niro, you better believe I wanted to mix it up with him . . . that acting muscle was aching–that muscle was yelling."

It's this poison-ivy reaction that's so akin to comic books and their peculiar charm, where characters fight and scream within a sea of exclamation marks, and then disappear in the very next panel. It's a child's world that's torn from the mind of a man who drinks Yoo-hoo and collects John Travolta dolls, who declares with all the arrogance of an imbecile on his first date that when he gets serious about a girl, he shows her *Rio Bravo,* "and she better fucking like it." But he's also kept a child's clarity and devotion, as if every scene he's shot, with all its fury and its desire to amaze, is meant to cover up that first death he encountered on the screen–Bambi's mom– a wound that will remain with all movie brats for the rest of our lives . . .

3.

Where does the Anchovy Bandit go next? He's written and directed the final two-hour episode for the 2004–2005 season of *CSI.* The Bandit's own contribution bears a curious resemblance to Beatrix buried alive in *Kill Bill;* in the finale of *CSI,* a Crime Scene investigator is buried in a glass coffin, but he hasn't studied with Pei Mai, and it's his mates who get him out of there. It's no surprise, since they have their own magic; like Tarantino himself they love Roy Rogers and Trigger and are obsessed with board games. "Trigger is the Uma Thurman of horses," according to Tarantino.

The Bandit also stole onto the set of Frank Miller and Robert Rodriguez's *Sin City* (based on Frank Miller's own comic-book characters) and directed a scene in which a dead man starts to talk despite the hatchet stuck in his head. I'm not the only one who saw a resemblance between *Sin City* and *Kill Bill,* between Rodriguez's hyperactive monsters and Tarantino's—ghosts on the move, hurling through time and space.

In "The Unreal Road from Toontown to 'Sin City,'" A. O. Scott tells us how "knowingly and ostentatiously deriv- ative" is Rodriguez's film. It's a symptom of "the global influence of Quentin Tarantino, whose genius as a director lies in his ability to recover, reanimate and recombine mori- bund and semi-obscure genres." The Bandit would prob- ably nod his head and agree with A. O. Scott. He sees himself as an illustrious grave robber, picking the bones of forgotten films. "I steal from every single movie ever made. I love it . . . I steal from everything. Great artists *steal,* they don't do *hommages*," he said at a press conference in Cannes, after he was accused of lifting *Reservoir Dogs* wholesale from Ringo Lam's *City on Fire.*

We'll have to forgive him for sounding like a two-bit Michelangelo—the Bandit was enraged. He had "borrowed" the basic story from Ringo Lam: an undercover cop embedded in a gang of thieves that rob a jewelry store in Hong Kong; the film ends with the same Mexican stand-off, the same unraveling of the thieves themselves. But there's no Mr. Blonde in *City of Fire,* at least no maniacal dance, no madcap dialogue, no toying with time. Tarantino might steal a particular shot: Chow Yun-Fat unloading a pair of pistols at the cops is similar to the target practice Mr. White and Pink take in confronting their own cops outside a phantom jewelry store. And there are no riffs in *City of Fire,* no breakdown of the narrative as Mr. Orange delivers his tale within a tale about bringing a bagful of weed into a toilet filled with cops.

Tarantino does "recover, reanimate, and recombine," but he also does something larger than that. He not only turns the moribund into a live monster, like some unholy cannibal, he gives us monsters we've never met before. And he reveals the skeleton of comic books in his every frame. . . .

Comic strips are as old as cinema itself, even older; the first American strips appeared just as immigrants from Eastern Europe began to flood Chicago and Cleveland and New York in the latter part of the nineteenth century; newspapers would battle each other in their Sunday supplements to grab the attention of greenhorns and other illiterates with "funnies" that featured brats with broken English, like the Katzenjammers or the Yellow Kid, whose nightshirt was both a message board and a word balloon; these early strips were about rebellious children for an audience that the newspapers themselves treated as children.

The comic books that grew out of such strips and began to flourish in the forties with a whole basket of heroes—Superman, Batman, Plastic Man, Wonder Woman, Sheena, Captain Marvel, etc.—were often created by the children of immigrants imagining an America of prodigious men and women, "immortal" mortals, who were only fantastic versions of themselves as warriors at the beginning of a new world war . . .

Comics were much bolder than any other form of art; by insisting upon a savage simplification, a world where children ruled, without much complication but with a boy's ability to have an undying crush on a particular babe (some Sheena who walked out of the jungle to break our heart), these inventors of comic books, these explorers, working in teams, or alone, could enter imaginative fields where more sophisticated grown-ups wouldn't have bothered to go; it was a world without gray areas, without ambiguity, where renegades hoped to rule—either mad old men like Dr. Sivana, or evil geniuses in their prime, like Lex Luthor, and clownish masterminds, like the Joker, or nimble connivers, like Catwoman.

The hidden truth of the comic book was that the gods of evil were much more clever and vivid than any gods of the good, and we paid more attention to these super villains than to the superheroes themselves. The war between good and evil could never end, or Batman would be out of business. There was something gloriously static about the hero's pursuits. Comics kept clear of the "roundness" and "depth" we demanded of other art. Comics were like deadly rockets that sabotaged our own complicated culture—they insisted on the narrow, the mean, the small.

The postmodern was born within the panels of a comic, where the decor could shift at any moment, where nothing was rational or safe, and the superhero was like some clockwork creature in a mask, more monstrous than the monsters he had to chase. If the comic book is addicted to surfaces and different decors, that's because it distrusts the notion of a center—it echoes the child's suspicion of causes and beliefs. It delights in panel by panel intrigue, in fun rather than meaning.

A. O. Scott can rightly say of *Sin City* (the film and the comic book) that it "offers sensation without feeling, death without grief, sin without guilt and, ultimately, novelty without surprise. Something is missing—something human." And he can with a certain bemusement prepare a casualty list for *Kill Bill Vol. 1:* "It has shootings, stabbings, beatings, beheadings, disembowelings, amputations, mutilations, eye-gougings, slicings, choppings, bitings and spanking. Also some naughty words."

But even with all the beatings and beheadings, Tarantino sculpts with his own fiery clay—his films are darker, funnier, and have more shape than anything Robert Rodriguez has ever done. If the Anchovy Bandit has a "global influence," it's because he's tapped into the childlike unconscious of other "children" sitting in the dark, forced them to look into the void, as if they were reliving the death of Bambi's mom with him, and he's filled frame after frame with a relentless energy that has kept them as willing prisoners.

No one can really predict how future generations will react to the Bandit and his films. Language changes so rapidly that what is in fashion right now may become unreadable. And as Tarantino moves from project to project, from one false start to the next, like any mogul, one has to admit that he's the ultimate movie monster, defending Asian flicks or reminiscing about some forgotten blaxploitation star, as if the memory of all cinema resided in him, as if he's wedded himself permanently to those shadows on the wall, and he himself is part shadow, part man and boy—the Anchovy Bandit who breaks into our dreams and goes on troubling us long after we've roused ourselves and risen from sleep.

Selected Bibliography

Agee, James. "Comedy's Greatest Era." *Life,* September 5, 1949.

Barthelme, Donald. "The Indian Uprising," in *Unspeakable Practices, Unnatural Acts.* New York: Farrar, Straus & Giroux, 1968. First appeared in *The New Yorker,* March 6, 1965.

Bazin, André. *Orson Welles: A Critical View.* Los Angeles: Acrobat Books, 1992.

Berger, Arthur Asa, ed. *The Postmodern Presence: Readings on Postmodernism in American Culture and Society.* Walnut Creek, CA: AltaMira Publishing, 1998.

Bernard, Jami. *Quentin Tarantino: The Man and His Movies.* New York: HarperPerennial, 1995.

Bhattacharya, Sanjiv. "Mr Blonde's Ambition." *The Observer,* April 18, 2004.

Biskind, Peter. *Down and Dirty Pictures: Miramax, Sundance, and the Rise of Independent Films.* New York: Simon & Schuster, 2004.

Braudy, Leo and Marshall Cohen. *Film Theory and Criticism.* Sixth Edition. New York: Oxford University Press, 2004.

Carringer, Robert L. *The Making of Citizen Kane.* Berkeley: University of California Press, 1985, 1996.

Carroll, Lewis. *Alice in Wonderland.* Donald J. Gray, ed. New York: W. W. Norton, 1971, 1992.

Chabon, Michael. *The Amazing Adventures of Kavalier & Clay.* New York: Random House, 2000.

Cooper, Denis. "Minor Magic." *ArtForum*, March 1995.

Coveney, Peter. "Escape," in Carroll.

Crouch, Stanley. "Eggplant Blues: The Miscegenated Cinema of Quentin Tarantino." Introd. to *Pulp Fiction*, Grove Press, 1994.

Dargis, Manohla. "Quentin Tarantino on *Pulp Fiction*," in Peary.

Dawson, Jeff. *Quentin Tarantino: The Cinema of Cool.* New York: Applause Books, 1995.

Ellroy, James. *My Dark Places.* New York: Alfred A. Knopf, 1996.

Empson, William. "The Child as Swain," in Carroll.

Farber, Manny. *Negative Space.* Reprint. New York: Da Capo Press, 1971, 1998.

Fleisher, Michael L. *The Great Superman Book.* New York: Warner Books, 1978.

Fleming, Michael. "Tarantino's Discovery Network." *Variety,* September 1–7, 1997.

Gitlin, Todd. "Postmodernism: Roots and Politics," in Berger. Reprinted from *Dissent,* Winter 1989.

Glieberman, Owen. "Knockout Bunch." *Entertainment Weekly,* October 7, 1994.

Hirschberg, Lynn. "The Two Hollywoods: the man who changed everything." *The New York Times,* November 16, 1997.

Hoberman, J. "Interview: Quentin Tarantino," in Peary.

hooks, bell. "Cool Tool." *ArtForum,* March 1995.

Hornaday, Ann. "Quentin Tarantino in Austin, Texas." *Austin American Statesman,* August 10, 1996.

Indiana, Gary. "Geek Chic." *ArtForum,* March 1995.

Kurtzman, Harvey. *From AARGH! To ZIP!: Harvey Kurtzman's Visual History of the Comics.* New York: Prentice Hall, 1991.

MacFarquhar, Larissa. "Profiles: The Movie Lover." *The New Yorker,* October 20, 2003.

Mendelsohn, Daniel. "It's Only A Movie." *The New York Review of Books,* December 18, 2003.

Mooney, Joshua. "Interview with Quentin Tarantino," in Peary.

Mulvey, Laura. "Visual Pleasure and Narrative Cinema," in Baudy. Reprinted from *Screen,* Volume 16, Number 23 (1975).

Nevers, Camille. "Encounter with Quentin Tarantino," in Peary.

Peary, Gerald, ed. *Quentin Tarantino Interviews.* Jackson: University Press of Mississippi, 1998.

Polan, Dana. *Pulp Fiction.* London: British Film Institute, 2000.

Pynchon, Thomas. *V.* Philadelphia: J. B. Lippincott, 1963.

Rodrick, Stephen. "Odd Man In." *The New York Times Magazine,* May 30, 2004.

Rose, Charlie. *The Charlie Rose Show.* PBS, October 14, 1994; December 26, 1997; April 22, 2004.

Schatzberg, Jerry. Interview, December 30, 2004.

Scott, A. O. "Blood Bath & Beyond." *The New York Times,* October 10, 2003.

—— "The Unreal Road from Toontown to 'Sin City.'" *The New York Times,* April 24, 2005.

Smith, Gavin. "When You Know You're in Good Hands," in Peary.

Tarantino, Quentin. *Pulp Fiction.* New York: Miramax Books, 1994.

——*Reservoir Dogs.* New York: Grove Press, 1994.

Taylor, Ella. "Quentin Tarantino's *Reservoir Dogs* and the Thrill of Excess," in Peary.

Wollen, Peter. From "Signs and Meaning in the Cinema, the Auteur Theory," in Braudy.

Wood, Robin. "Slick Shtick." *ArtForum,* March 1995.

Woods, Paul A. *King Pulp: The Wild World of Quentin Tarantino.* London: Plexus Publishing, 1998.

Notes

Introduction

xxviii.   "I love the way": Peary, p. 57.

xxviii.   "[Jean] Renoir once remarked": Braudy and Cohen,
          p. 575.

xxix.   "To spend time": Peary, p. 154.

xxix.   "To me there is": Dawson, p. 53.

xxx.   "He's a genius": Bernard, p. 16.

xxx.   "Robert Mitchum was on a balcony": Peary, p. 28.

xxx.   "I'm not ragging": Peary, p. 52.

xxxi.   "no flashbacks, just chapters": Peary, p. 7.

xxxii.   "a lot more resonance": October 14, 1994.

xxxiii.   "a frightened and rather": Ellroy, *My Dark Places*, p. 70.

xxxiii.   "I hated her": Ellroy, p. 101.

xxxiii.   "Every book I read": Ellroy, p. 116.

xxxiv.   "We were poor": Ellroy, p. 129.

xxxiv.   "I was a Method actor": Ellroy, pp. 147–148.

xxxiv.   "Burglary was voyeurism": Ellroy, p. 159.

xxxiv.   "Jail was my health retreat": Ellroy, p. 173.

xxxiv.   "It was like trying": Ellroy, p. 183.

xxxiv.   "I possessed a self-preserving streak": Ellroy, p. 248.

xxxiv.   "I didn't know that storytelling": Ellroy, p. 153.

xxxv.   "I wanted to canonize": Ellroy, p. 252.

xxxv.   "I was hassled": Bernard, p. 159.

xxxv.   "a combination of Elvis": Bernard, p. 143.

xxxv.   "If I hadn't wanted": Peary", p. xiv.

xxxvi.   "I–I only have a mom": Peary, p. 75.

xxxvi.   "I never met": Peary, p. 121.

xxxvi.   [Quentin's] like *me*": Bernard, p. 9.

xxxvii.   "Quentin came out": Bernard, p. 200.

xxxviii. "Quentin's strength comes": Dawson, p. 22.

xxxviii. "I don't know how": Peary, p. 64.

xxxviii. "all chicken scratch": Bernard, p. 219.

Chapter One

5. "I *am* half Cherokee": Dawson, p. 17.
5. "Quentin will have you believe": Bernard, p. 5.
5. "[Quentin's] always driving": Bernard, p. 10.
5. "I can't find his fear": Peary, p. 126.
6. "Violence was like": Charlie Rose, October 14, 1994.
6. "you're at the funny part": Woods, p. 12.
6. "I like the idea": Peary, p. 31.
7. [. . .] my mother was always": Bernard, p. 6.
7. "Everyone else was": Bernard, p. 7.
8. "I was so angry": Bernard, p. 7.
8. "I decided when I was pregnant": Bernard, p. 8.
11. "He loved kindergarten": Bernard, p. 19.
11. "Something misfired there": Bernard, p. 16.
11. "When I saw *Pulp Fiction*": Woods, p. 11.
12. It wasn't me": Bernard, p. 11.
13. "You didn't want to go": Biskind, p. 122.
14. "It was at the point": Dawson, p. 23.
14. "one of the greatest": Charlie Rose, October 14, 1994.
15. ". . . little by little": Peary, pp. 11–12.
15. "It was so cool": Peary, p. 12.
15. "just surfaced every once": Bernard, p. 53.
15. "this little stupid job": Charlie Rose, October 14, 1994.
15. "a magnet for every": Biskind, p. 127.
16. "He came by as a film buff ": Dawson, p. 30.
16. "I basically lived there": Peary, p. 131.
16. "like an exotic butterfly": Biskind, p. 130.
16. "Every year I'd get": Bernard, p. 12.
17. "He had no concept": Bernard, p. 30.
17. "This is one of the few places": Woods, p. 11.
17. "I like to read": Peary, p. 160.
17. "I've read everything": Peary, p. 13.

18.   "Why go to film school": Biskind, p. 127.

19.   "a culture of scarcity": Biskind, p. 127.

19.   "stripping film of its hieratic halo": Biskind, p. 127.

19.   "There's a fresh generation": Peary, p. 131.

19.   "most accomplished practitioner": Biskind, p. 127.

21.   "square dance": Peary, p. 43.

21.   "Now Video Archives": Peary, p. 31.

21.   "show a high regard": Bernard, p. 183.

22.   "a big, brawny": Peary, p. 71.

22.   "He could sell you": Dawson, p. 32.

22.   "An only child": Bernard, p. 171.

22.   "no sense of style": Biskind, p. 314.

22.   "should go to movie jail": Peary, p. 96.

23.   "Everything for Carroll": Carroll, p. 329.

23.   "He was as fond of me": Carroll, p. 304.

24.   "his face became girlish": Carroll, p. 329.

24.   "when Sin and Sorrow": Carroll, p. 282.

24.   "embodiment of ungovernable passion": Carroll, p. 282.

24.   "the Queen of Hearts": Carroll, p. 344.

Chapter Two

29.   "wrote things to sell": Peary, p. 3.

30.   "we had the exact": Peary, p. 131.

30.   "sort of this invisible character": Peary, p. 21.

30.   "guitar picks": Charlie Rose, October 14, 1994.

31.   "sometimes C.O.D": Bernard, p. 65.

33.   "We were both very broke": Woods, p. 25.

33.   "the delicate features of a dancer": Bernard, p. 121.

33.   "I was going to become": Bernard, p. 122.

34.   "All of a sudden": Woods, p. 26.

35.   "You make a movie": Peary, p. 28.

36.   "We were struggling": Bernard, p. 133.

37.   "pure cinema": Dawson, p. 58.

37.   "I didn't use storyboards": Peary, p. 18.

38.   "He's an older guy": Peary, p. 27.

43.   "the suffocating, claustrophobic space": Peary, p. 6.

44.   "Jim Thompson meets": Dawson, p. 64.

45.   "It's a syrup": Dawson, p. 62.

45.   "It's under a freeway": Dawson, pp. 59–60.

47.   "The torture scene infuriates me": Peary, p. 47.

47.   "The cinema isn't intruding": Peary, p. 46.

47.   "I like fucking with": "The Movie Lover," p. 155.

47.   "You're supposed to laugh": Peary, p. 46.

47.   [Y]ou're tapping your toe": Dawson, p. 81.

48.   "That's what Mr. Blonde": Dawson, p. 83.

49.   "I'm trying to wipe out": Dawson, p. 42.

50.   "Without this scene": Biskind, p. 135.

50.   "I try to explain": Peary, p. 63.

52.   "For the rest of my life": Bernard, p. 152.

53.   "It was completely wild": Dawson, p. 64.

54.   "like an actor would": Bernard, p. 166.

54.   "And the only reason": Dawson, p. 173.

54.   "despite a hurricane of press": Biskind, p. 136.

54.   "What they did was": Bernard, p. 163.

55.   "Well, as you know": Bernard, p. 147.

55.   "It's an expression used": Peary, p. 14.

55.   "was that it sounds like": Peary, p. 14.

56.   "To make a film": Biskind, p. 24.

57.   "I don't fight": Peary, p. 165.

57.   "may have loved Godard": Biskind, p. 120.

57.   "What I really wanted": Peary, p. 81.

58.   "I mean it was absurd": Dawson, p. 79.

58.   "There is no blood": Peary, p. 74.

Chapter Three

61.   "[e]very film should be better": Peary, p. 7.

61.   "The razzle-dazzle came": Peary, p. 200.

61.   "nearly a million dollars": Dawson, p. 140.

61.   "like old girlfriends": Peary, p. 51.

62.   "Even though the movie": Peary, p. 64.

62.   "one of the subtexts": Polan, p. 42.

63.   "the thirty years": "The Movie Lover," p. 159.

64.   "There are a bunch": Peary, p. 81.

64.   "[I]n the course of time": Bernard, p. 173.

65.   "Quentin is a brilliant guy": Bernard, p. 118.

65.   "paid me a lot of money": Dawson, p. 148.

65.   "Miramax went into overdrove": Biskind, p. 156.

66.   "an $8 million chance": Bernard, p. 2.

66.   Miramax is in the Quentin Tarantino business":
        Bernard, p. 2.

66.   "Expect the unexpected": Bernard, p. 4.

66.   "the two slobs": Biskind, p. 153.

66.   "300 pounds and counting": Biskind, p. 13.

66.   "He tore phones": Biskind, p. 69.

67.   "They were good and evil": Biskind, p. 72.

67.   "If I didn't exist": Biskind, p. 25.

67.   "In the studio world": Biskind, p. 1.

68.   "He's working class": Bernard, p. 234.

68.   "And when Harvey pushes": Bernard, p. 197.

68.   "I was kind of moved": Bernard, p. 197.

69.   "I wasn't sure that": Peary, p. 120.

69.   "I think I was the only one": Bernard, p. 198.

69.   "One of the reasons": Peary, p. 165.

73.   "They are friends in real life": Peary, pp. 83–84.

73.   "Tim Roth is a very fine actor": "The Two Hollywoods."

74.   "Tarantino doesn't so much": Peary, p. 45.

74.   "I found it rather terrifying": Bernard, p. 191.
75.   "lying, cheating lapdog": Polan, p. 61.
76.   "a dorky white boy": Polan, p. 63.
78.   "I sat down": Woods, p. 106.

Chapter Four

81.   "a sense of terrain": Farber, p. 9.
81.   "[A] movie filled with negative space": Farber, p. 10.
82.   "separate the actor": Bazin, p. 80.
83.   "an art form": Peary, p. 163.
86.   "realities tumble into one another": introduction to *Reservoir Dogs*, p. xiii.
95.   "At the end of the day": Woods, p. 200.
96.   "*Pulp Fiction* posse": Dawson, p. 116.
96.   "fans made a fuss": Bernard, p. 209.
96.   "some gorefest": Dawson, p. 167.
97.   "it was as if a fairy": Biskind, p. 79.
97.   "You can't fuck around": Bernard, p. 211.
98.   "There was a certain amount": Bernard, p. 211.
98.   "and no one believed it": "The Two Hollywoods".
99.   "You can't just change": Bernard, p. 97.
99.   "To me the best thing": Woods, p. 138.
100.   "In Europe and everywhere": Bernard, p. 79.
100.   "The question is": Bernard, p. 100.
100.   "I've never seen": Dawson, p. 12.
101.   "became a god overnight": Bernard, p. 103.
102.   "After *Pulp Fiction*": Peary, p. 156.
102.   "it ended up": Peary, pp. 192–193.
103.   "I am so happy": Bernard, p. 202.
103.   "I mean, I'm really": Polan, p. 81.
107.   "We spent a good part": Peary, p. 86.
108.   "Quentin is not Jimmy Stewart": Biskind, p. 315.

108.   "the whole treasure of the movies": Peary, p. 87.
109.   "Marlon Brando and Michael Caine": Peary, p. 87.

Chapter Five

113.   "We showed *Pulp Fiction*": Woods, p. 174.
113.   "the video piracy": Peary, p. 182.
113.   "Life's just too short": Dawson, p. 11.
114.   "I remember when I was younger": Woods, p. 146.
114.   "the busiest hiatus": Woods, p. 146.
114.   "[H]e relishes the challenge": Woods, p. 159.
115.   "like making a film": Woods, p. 155.
115.   "When you work with Quentin": Woods, pp. 154–155.
116.   "fifth auteur": Woods, p. 156.
116.   "ended up shouldering": Peary, p. 149.
117.   "These prints are like": Hornaday, "Quentin Tarantino in Austin, Texas."
117.   "turned into a week": Hornaday.
117.   "What tickles me": Hornaday.
119.   "No, no, no, I'm not gonna": Peary, p. 171.
119.   "He already sees himself": Bernard, p. 189.
119.   "I became an adjective": "The Two Hollywoods".
119.   "I did not want it": Woods, p. 182.
123.   "a long, plaited goatee beard": Woods, p. 189.
124.   "is about getting to know": Woods, p. 188.
124.   "Every two or three years": "The Movie Lover."
127.   "has worked her way down": Woods, p. 193
127.   "come on with no make-up": Woods, p. 185.
128.   "giving second [and third]": *Variety*, September 1–7, 1997.
128.   "Robert Forster's face": "The Movie Lover, p. 150.
129.   "The last five years": Fleming, "Tarantino's Discovery Network."
129.   "A lot of these actors": "Tarantino's Discovery Network."

Chapter Six

133. "You can't lose": Woods, p. 200.
143. "may be a tongue-in-cheek nod": "Blood Bath & Beyond."
143. "Answers first, questions later": Peary, p. 7.
147. "a whole city, an entire civilization": Agee, "Comedy's Greatest Era."
147. "severed limbs and writhing trunks": "Blood Bath & Beyond."
158. "the strangest, wackiest planet": Fleisher, p. 21.
159. The Bizarro World": Fleisher, p. 21.

Finale

170. "I dreamed we had finished": Bernard, p. 200.
172. "the desperate air": Polan, p. 63.
174. "I ate. I drank": Bernard, p. 204.
174. "I get a chance": Peary, p. 30.
174. "You have heard of method acting": Woods, p. 186.
174. "I had to really work hard": Woods, p. 186.
175. [I]f I didn't act": Peary, p. 212.
175. "and she better fucking like it": Peary, p. 133.
176. "Trigger is the Uma Thurman": Biskind, p. 314.
176. "I steal from every single": Dawson, p. 91.